编委会

一流高职院校旅游大类创新型人才培养"十三五"规划教材

顾问

郑 焱　　湖南师范大学教授、博士生导师
　　　　　湖南省旅游首席专家团专家

许春晓　　湖南省旅游研究院常务副院长
　　　　　湖南师范大学旅游学院副院长，教授、博士生导师

总主编

江 波　　湖南省职业教育与成人教育学会高职旅游类专业委员会秘书长，教授

编委 （排名不分先后）

陈 朝　　陈晓斌　　韩燕平　　刘韵琴　　李 蓉
皮 晖　　覃业银　　王志凡　　伍 欣　　肖 炜
叶 宏　　余 芳　　翟 丽

一流高职院校旅游大类创新型人才培养"十三五"规划教材

总主编⊙江 波

旅游实用英语

Practical English for Tourism

主　编 ◎ 叶　宏　　郭红芳　　柳　波
副主编 ◎ 胡晓青　　孔　瑢　　许艳平　　何　姗　　白扬易
参　编 ◎ 罗思静　　雷长青　　钟　真　　李　琨　　郑　翔
　　　　刘　权

华中科技大学出版社
http://www.hustp.com
中国·武汉

内 容 简 介

本书紧跟国际化人才培养的步伐,始终贯彻"以职业为中心,以就业为先导"的理念,采用项目任务驱动法、体验式教学法、互动式教学法,以灵活多样、有趣实用的内容设计,配以外籍专业人士的录音,突出英语听、说、读、写全方位的语言能力训练。本书在分析入境旅游活动全过程和旅行社入境旅游团接待服务全过程的基础上,通过解构涉外导游服务流程、涉外旅游服务岗位能力要求设计而成。

本书既可作为高职高专旅游类专业的专用教材,也可作为旅游服务人员的学习用书和旅游企业的培训用书。

图书在版编目(CIP)数据

旅游实用英语/叶宏,郭红芳,柳波主编.—武汉:华中科技大学出版社,2018.8(2020.8重印)
一流高职院校旅游大类创新型人才培养"十三五"规划教材
ISBN 978-7-5680-4376-2

Ⅰ.①旅… Ⅱ.①叶… ②郭… ③柳… Ⅲ.①旅游-英语-高等职业教育-教材 Ⅳ.①F59

中国版本图书馆 CIP 数据核字(2018)第 203855 号

旅游实用英语　　　　　　　　　　　　　　　　　　叶　宏　郭红芳　柳　波　主编
Lüyou Shiyong Yingyu

策划编辑:周　婵
责任编辑:刘　平
封面设计:杨小川
责任校对:李　琴
责任监印:周治超

出版发行:华中科技大学出版社(中国·武汉)　　电话:(027)81321913
　　　　　武汉市东湖新技术开发区华工科技园　　邮编:430223
录　　排:华中科技大学惠友文印中心
印　　刷:武汉市籍缘印刷厂
开　　本:787mm×1092mm　1/16
印　　张:16.5　插页:2
字　　数:392 千字
版　　次:2020 年 8 月第 1 版第 2 次印刷
定　　价:42.00 元

本书若有印装质量问题,请向出版社营销中心调换
全国免费服务热线:400-6679-118　竭诚为您服务
版权所有　侵权必究

总 序

全域旅游时代,旅游业作为国民经济战略性支柱产业与改善民生的幸福产业,对拉动经济增长与满足人民美好生活需要起着重要作用。2016年,我国旅游业总收入达4.69万亿元,旅游业对国民经济综合贡献率高达11%,对社会就业综合贡献率超过10.26%,成为经济转型升级与全面建成小康社会的重要推动力。"十三五"期间,我国旅游业将迎来新一轮黄金发展期,旅游业消费大众化、需求品质化、竞争国际化、发展全域化、产业现代化等发展趋势将对旅游从业人员的数量与质量提出更高的要求。因此,如何培养更多适合行业发展需要的高素质旅游人才成为旅游职业教育亟待解决的问题。

2015年,国家旅游局联合教育部发布《加快发展现代旅游职业教育的指导意见》,提出要"加快构建现代旅游职业教育体系,培养适应旅游产业发展需求的高素质技术技能和管理服务人才",标志着我国旅游职业教育进入了重要战略机遇期。同年,教育部新一轮的职业教育目录调整,为全国旅游职业教育专业群发展提供了切实指引。高职院校专业群建设有利于优化专业结构、促进资源整合、形成育人特色。随着高职教学改革的逐渐深入,专业群建设已成为高职院校迈向一流的必经之路。教材建设是高职院校的一项基础性工作,也是衡量学校办学水平的重要标志。正是基于旅游大类职业教育变革转型的大背景以及高职院校"争创一流"的时机,出版一套"一流高职院校旅游大类创新型人才培养'十三五'规划教材"成为当前旅游职业教育发展的现实需要。

为此,我们集中了一大批高水平的旅游职业院校的学科专业带头人和骨干教师以及资深业界专家等,共同编写了本套教材。

本套教材的编写力争适应性广、实用性强、有所创新和超越,具备以下几方面的特点。

一是定位精准,具备区域特色。教材定位在一流高职培养层次,依托高职旅游专业群,突出实用、适用、够用和创新"三用一新"的特点。教材编写立足湖南实际,在编写中融入湖南地方特色,以服务于区域旅游大类专业的建设与发展。

二是教材建设系统化。本套教材计划分批推出30本,涵盖目前高等职业院校旅游大类开设的大部分专业课程和院校特色课程。

三是校企合作一体化。教材由各高职院校专业带头人、青年骨干教师、旅游业内专家组成编写团队,他们教学与实践经验丰富,保证了教材的品质。

四是配套资源立体化。本套教材强化纸质教材与数字化资源的有机结合,构建了配套的教学资源库,包括教学课件、案例库、习题集、视频库等教学资源。强调线上线下互为配套,打造独特的立体教材。

希望通过这套以"一流高职院校旅游大类创新型人才培养"为目标的教材的编写与出版,为我国高职高专旅游大类教育的教材建设探索一套"能显点,又盖面;既见树木,又见森林"的教材编写和出版模式,并希望本套教材能成为具有时代性、规范性、示范性和指导性,优化配套的、具有专业针对性和学科应用性的一流高职院校旅游大类教育的教材体系。

湖南省职业教育与成人教育学会
高职旅游类专业委员会秘书长
湖南省教学名师
江波　教授
2017 年 11 月

前言

随着"一带一路"倡议的深入发展,旅游产业迈入了发展新轨道,更多的国际游客将前来领略中国之美。《旅游实用英语》一书正是紧跟国际化人才培养的步伐,紧贴涉外旅游服务岗位要求编写而成。本教材既可作为高职高专旅游类专业的专用教材,也可广泛用于旅游服务人员自学和旅游企业培训。

全书通过解构涉外导游服务流程、涉外旅游服务岗位能力要求,选取了13个主要任务模块,内容涵盖了从旅游咨询服务到送站服务的涉外旅游服务全过程,设计新颖实用,可操作性强,其特色表现如下。

1. 融入湖南地方特色

在研究分析已有教材的优缺点基础上,立足湖南实际,设计了一个英国孔子学院旅游团在湖南长沙-韶山3天2晚的旅游接待任务,在教材编写中充分融入湖南地方特色,有效服务于区域旅游大类专业的建设与发展。

2. 内容设计基于两个过程

本书在分析入境旅游活动全过程和旅行社入境旅游团接待服务全过程两个方面的基础上,形成了涵盖旅游咨询、接受任务、入境和通关、接站、赴饭店途中服务、入住饭店、核对与商定日程、餐饮服务、参观游览、旅游交通、旅游购物、旅游娱乐、送站服务等13个任务模块,环环相扣,既是入境旅游团一次完整的旅游活动,又是旅行社一次完整的国际旅游团接待服务活动。

3. 任务驱动,实用性强

全书采用一个入境旅游团接待任务贯穿全书,每个任务模块对应国际旅行社完成该入境旅游团接待任务的一个环节,学习结束意味着此次国际旅游团接待任务圆满结束。

每个项目任务的学习设计了"任务导入—任务解析—任务拓展—知识链接"4个步骤,思路清晰明了,内容对接工作实际,能直接、有效地帮助学习者掌握专业知识与技能。

4. 突出"体验式""互动式"教学特色

始终贯彻"以职业为中心,以就业为先导"的理念,设计了看图填写、选择、匹配、排序、填表、听力、翻译、模拟、阅读等多种形式的拓展任务,营造"体验式""互动式"的学习环境,突出英语听、说、读、写全方位的语言能力训练。

本教材由湖南省多所一流职业院校骨干教师编写。叶宏(湖南外贸职业学院)、郭红芳

(湖南外贸职业学院)、柳波(湖南网络工程职业学院)担任主编,负责教材大纲编写和全书审稿、统稿、修改、编排工作;胡晓青、孔瑢、许艳平、何姗、白扬易担任副主编。郭红芳负责编写模块四、模块五;湖南交通职业技术学院孔瑢负责编写模块十二;湖南民族职业学院白扬易负责编写模块一、模块十;邵阳职业技术学院许艳平负责编写模块七、模块九、模块十一;湖南外贸职业学院何姗负责编写模块二、模块六,罗思静负责编写模块三,胡晓青负责编写模块十三,雷长青负责编写模块八。湖南外贸职业学院钟真、李琨、郑翔、刘权参与了资料的收集、整理、文字校对等工作。

中国旅游业蓬勃发展,变化日新月异,旅游者需求多种多样,本教材难免有疏漏和不妥之处,敬请各位行家、学者和读者不吝批评指正。

目 录

Module 1 Travel Information

Task 1 Recommending tourism products /2
Task 2 Answering tourists' queries /5

Module 2 Receiving Tasks

Task 1 Familiar with the plan /18
Task 2 Reconfirm the arrangement /23
Task 3 Preparations for meeting a tour group /27

Module 3 Immigration and Customs

Task 1 Check in at the airport /34
Task 2 Go through the immigration /36
Task 3 Go through the customs /39

Module 4 Meeting Guests

Task 1 Meet the tour group /44
Task 2 Meet a FIT guest /48

Module 5 On the Way to the Hotel

Task 1 Extending a welcome speech /60
Task 2 Adjusting to the time difference /62
Task 3 Guiding on the Way /64
Task 4 Warm reminding /71

Module 6 At the Hotel

Task 1 Checking in /82
Task 2 Introducing Hotel Facilities /86
Task 3 Wake-up Call /90

Module 7 Talking about the Itinerary

- Task 1 Discussing the Itinerary /98
- Task 2 Handling Changes in the Itinerary /102

Module 8 At the Restaurant

- Task 1 Booking Tables /112
- Task 2 Dining at a Chinese Restaurant /114
- Task 3 Dining at a Western restaurant /117
- Task 4 Tasting Local Food /120

Module 9 Visiting Scenic Spots

- Task 1 City Sightseeing /128
- Task 2 Cultural Landscape /131
- Task 3 Natural Landscape /134

Module 10 Transportation

- Task 1 Public Transportation /144
- Task 2 Rent a Car /146

Module 11 Shopping in Tourism

- Task 1 Souvenirs /154
- Task 2 Arts and Crafts /157
- Task 3 Tea /160

Module 12 Recreational Program

- Task 1 Health Activities /168
- Task 2 Watch Shows /170
- Task 3 Pubs and Bars /172
- Task 4 Traditional Chinese Entertainment /175

Module 13 Seeing off Guests

- Task 1 Checking Out /186
- Task 2 Extending a Farewell Speech /190
- Task 3 Departure Procedure /193

Keys for Reference /200
References /251

Module 1
Travel Information

Nowadays, it is very common for people to take holidays and weekends when travelling. There are many ways in which you can get information about an intended destination. The most convenient way is from a travel agency. As a travel agency clerk or a tour guide, when guests come to your travel agency, you should be able to recommend tourism products and answer their queries. You should do a good job to introduce featured tour packages of your agency to them, or recommend your excellent packages according to their requirements, and sometimes even design some new packages for the guests based on their specific requirements. As well, you have to answer their questions on the travel time, destinations, visiting places, food, transportation, accommodation, entertainment and so on.

◇ Learning Objectives

Knowledge

① Learn how to introduce tourism products to the guests.

② Know the information of food, transportation, accommodation and entertainment of travel destinations.

③ Master the vocabulary and expressions about tourism products.

Skills

① Be able to introduce tourism products.

② Be able to answer the guest's questions at the travel agency.

Quality

① Be polite and patient to the guests.

② Develop service consciousness.

③ Strengthen communication ability.

Task 1 Recommending tourism products

◇Lead-in

A group of the British Confucius Institute teachers and students is planning to go on a tour to China. Their leader Susan came to CITS (China International Travel Service) for help. Kevin, the clerk of CITS, received Susan.

◇Analyzing the Task

Kevin can recommend a travel package as following.

① Have a thorough understanding and knowledge of the tourism products in the travel agency.

② Greet the guests warmly, seat them and offer tea or coffee.

③ Ask for the guests' needs.

④ Introduce the travel packages concisely.

⑤ Present brochures promptly when the guests are interested.

⑥ Bid a farewell politely.

The on-the-spot communication is as following.

(C=the clerk of CITS   L=the leader of the British Confucius Institute)

C: Good morning, sir. Welcome to China International Travel Service. What can I do for you?

L: I'd like to look at some travel packages.

C: No problem. Here is our travel brochure. Well, where are you going?

L: Can you tell me the popular sightseeing route?

C: Since you are from Britain, I recommend Changsha-Shaoshan, a two-day-and-three-night tour. Shaoshan is Chairman Mao's hometown, which is one of the hottest places of interest in China. There are thousands of people visiting there every day. And being the capital city of Hunan, Changsha owns a lot of places of interest which have historical significance.

L: I admire Chairman Mao very much. I have heard a lot of him.

C: Here are several brochures for you.

L: Could you please tell me if the price you have offered in the brochure covers all the expenses?

C: Yes, but not including the items at your own expense. Would you like to go over the itinerary?

L: Yes, please.

C: On the first day, the tour group will have a full day tour to Changsha City, including visiting Yuelu Academy, Orange Island, the Museum of Hunan Province and the Xiang Embroidery Museum. On the second day, a bus will take you to Shaoshan to visit the former residence of Chairman Mao and Statue Square in the morning, and the Drop Water Tunnel in the afternoon. Then you'll go back to Changsha.

L: How about the dining?

C: Two special lunches, in the Changsha Fire Palace Restaurant and the Restaurant of Mao's, they are famous and the food is rather delicious.

L: Sounds interesting. How much should I pay for this package?

C: 568 RMB, not including the items at your own expense.

L: OK, I'll take it. Thank you and you are really helpful.

C: Wish you a nice trip.

Developing Tasks

1. Please choose the correct words for the sentences.

agency   accommodation   tour   group   depart

① Please recommend a _____ package to us.

② Welcome to our travel _____.

③ How many people are there in your _____?

④ We will _____ on Jul. 23.

⑤ Which _____ do you prefer, motel or resort?

2. Role play. Please act out the following dialogue.

Miss White, the group leader, is booking a group tour for her team.

The Staff should:

- Greet Miss White.
- Recommend a tourist destination.
- Ask the number of the people.
- Ask the departure time.
- Suggest a tour package.
- Offer a price.
- Confirm the reservation.

Miss White should:

- Book a group tour to the mountain.
- Tell the number of the team.
- Tell the departure time—this weekend; must come back before 4 p.m., Sunday.
- Choose a tour package, including 3 meals a day.
- Ask the price; want a discount.
- Express thanks and confirm the booking.

3. Listen and fill in the blanks.

(1) Complete the dialogue.

A: Good morning. ①_____?

B: Good morning. I'd like to go to ②_____. Could you recommend a ③_____ for me?

A: Sure. We have a tour package to Changsha ④_____. Here is the brochure.

B: That's fine. Is there free time for shopping?

A: Yes. You will have ⑤_____.

B: That's good. I will take this tour. How much is it?

A: ⑥_____. Including fees and tickets of ⑦_____.

B: OK. I want to book one for ⑧_____.

A: How many people are there in your party?

B: ⑨_____.

A: May I know your name and telephone number, please?

B: ⑩_____, and you can call me at ⑪_____.

A: OK. Let me confirm your reservation. You have booked ⑫_____. If there is no problem, please pay 800 Yuan.

B: OK.

(2) Listen again and decide whether the statements are true (T) or false (F).

① (　) Mr. Li is going to Changsha to spend his summer holiday.

② (　) The staff introduces a two-day-one-night tour package for Mr. Li.

③ (　) The tour will start on Saturday and end on Sunday.

④ (　) Mr. Li will go on the trip with his family.

⑤ (　) The clerk gives a discount to Mr. Li.

⑥ (　) Mr. Li will go shopping this Saturday night.

Task 2　Answering tourists' queries

Susan has many ideas and questions about this tour. How could Kevin answer the questions?

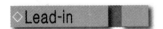

Kevin should:

① Have a thorough understanding and knowledge of the tourism products in the travel agency. Maintain and update the tourism information.

② Provide accurate information to the guests in a clear, courteous and professional manner.

③ Utilize communication skills to exceed the guests' expectation and increase revenue.

- Be well-groomed, show a cordial smile, and be patient at all times.

- Establish a rapport and trust with the guests at the first time.

- Know how to handling the guests' complaints.

④ Carry out work following the SOP laid down by the travel agency.

The on-the-spot communication is as following.

C: Good morning, madam, CITS. How can I help you?

L: Yes, I'd like to book a group tour to China.

C: OK, no problem. May I know how many people there are in your group?

L: 20 in total including 12 male and 8 female.

C: Which kind of tour do you prefer?

L: We are teachers and students of the British Confucius Institute. We are thinking about choosing an interesting and historical place for our holiday. Could you recommend one?

C: Yes. How about Hunan Province? There are famous Yuelu Academy and Chairman Mao's hometown. We have several tour packages here. You can have a look at the brochure. Here you are.

L: Thank you. Let me see. I'm interested in your five-day-four-night tour by air. How much is it?

C: This is our best package with 30% discount now. The price is 1,200 pound per person.

L: What are included in the charges?

C: Fees for transportation, accommodate, meals and entry to the tourist sites.

L: Oh, I see. That sounds great! Please reserve this trip for us.

C: Yes. Which day do you prefer to go?

L: We'd like to depart on Oct. 7, 2016.

C: That's fine. This tour package includes three meals a day. Does anyone have a special require for food in your group?

L: I don't know. I will ask them and phone you no later than tomorrow.

C: That will be great, thank you.

L: You're welcome.

C: May I have your name and contact number, please?

L: Susan Stone. 13907306978.

C: OK. Let me confirm your reservation. You have booked a five-day-four-night group tour for a group of 20 people to Hunan Province, China, in the name of Susan Stone. You will depart on Oct. 7 and back to London on Oct. 11. If there is no problem, please pay 10,000 pounds deposit.

L: Yes. Here is the card.

C: Thank you. Please sign here.

L: OK, here you are.

C: Please complete the reservation form.

L: OK, here you are.

C: Thank you. Here is your copy. If you change your mind, please notify us as soon as you can.

L: Fine. Thank you for your help. Goodbye!

C: My pleasure. Goodbye

◇Developing Tasks

1. Complete the dialogue.

(A＝the clerk   B＝the tourist)

A: Good morning. ①_____?（请问有什么能帮您的吗？）

B: Good morning. I want to go to an interesting place to spend the holiday.

A: ②_____?（请问您一行几人？）

B: Three in total, my wife, daughter and I.

A: ③_____?（请问你们想在那待几天？）

B: About three days.

A: OK. How about Changsha? You can visit the Museum of Hunan Province.

B: That sounds great! Do you have a 3-day tour package to Changsha?

A: Yes. ④_____.（请看我们的宣传册）

B: I like this tour package. How much is it?

A: 800 Yuan per person.

B: What are included in your charges?

A: ⑤_____.（交通费、住宿费、餐费、门票费）

B: ⑥_____?（有折扣吗?）

A: I'm sorry. ⑦_____.（四个人以上才有折扣）

B: I see. I will go back and discuss with my family.

A: Fine. ⑧_____.（您可以拨打我们的电话来确认预订）

B: That's OK. Thank you very much.

A: My pleasure.

2. Role play.

Situation One

The guest wants to have a four-day group tour to Beijing. Please perform a dialogue in group. You must use the words below.

flight ticket   tour package   20% discount   group tour

the Summer Palace

Situation Two

The guest has learnt the tour package on the Internet and interested in a five-day package to Shanghai. Please perform a dialogue in group. You must use the words below.

breakfast   by air   Shanghai Oriental Pearl TV Tower   five people

local food

3. Listen and fill in the blanks.

(1) Listen to the first part and answer the questions.

① Where would they spend the holiday?

② How many people are there in their party?

③ When is the departure date?

④ How much is the total travel expense for the family?

⑤ How many nights would they stay in Beijing?

(2) Listen to the second part and decide whether the statements are true (T) or false (F).

① (   ) The woman's surname is Stone.

② (   ) Her daughter cannot get the 50% discount.

③ (   ) Mrs. Stone's contact number is 13765298308.

（3）Listen to the third part and complete the dialogue.

B：OK. Mrs. Stone. You reserved ①_____. You have to pay ②_____.

A：No problem.

B：③_____?

A：Credit card.

B：④_____.

A：I have a Master Card. Here you are.

B：Thank you. ⑤_____.

A：OK.

B：⑥_____. Please keep it well.

A：Thank you very much.

B：⑦_____.

◇Related Knowledge

1. Major types of tour guides.

tour manager/tour escort 领队

national guide 全陪

local tour guide 地陪

scenic-spot guide 景点导游员

professional tour guide 职业导游员

non-professional tour guide/ amateur tour guide 非职业导游员

2. Package tour & DIY tour.

	Package tour	DIY tour
Advantages	• More convenient, saving much time and effort • More economical • Safer • More enjoyable	• More freedom • Fully appreciating the sights • More educational • Better chance to mix with local people • It's up to you when and where to shop or whether to shop at all.

续表

	Package tour	DIY tour
Disadvantages	• Less choice • Always in a hurry • Less educational • Too many shopping stops	• Inconvenient • Comparatively costly • May not be safe • Less enjoyable unless you have done your homework beforehand

3. An FIT holiday booking.

Smith wants to have a tour to spend his weekend. He comes to CITS.

(A=Smith   B=the staff)

B: Good morning. Welcome to CITS. How can I help you?

A: Good morning. I'd like to book a tour for this weekend.

B: Where would you like to go?

A: I want to go to Yueyang to spend my weekend. Is there a tour group that I can go with?

B: Yes. There is a tour group to Yueyang this weekend. Here is the brochure.

A: Thank you. I will book this tour.

B: OK. How many people are there in your party?

A: Just one.

B: I'm afraid you have to pay the extra fee for the hotel room.

A: Why?

B: We will book standard room for tourists, two persons per room. So you have to pay the fee for the extra bed in your room.

A: I see. How much do I owe you?

B: It's 600 yuan for the tour and 120 yuan for the extra bed. There is 720 yuan in total.

A: Can I get a discount?

B: This is a special rate.

A: Fine. Here is 720 yuan.

B: Thank you. Please confirm the reservation form and sign here.

A: OK. Thanks for your help.

B: My pleasure.

4. Key points of tour package promotion.

- Destinations

A good tour package should have at least one or several destinations. The destinations' history, culture and famous places are very important for the guests to choose the package. So the clerk of the travel agency has to get knowledge about different destinations.

- Visiting places

During the tour, most time is used to visit places. A good introduction of the visiting places will help you promote the package. The visiting places may be nature wonders as rivers or mountains, city buildings, historical sites, or cultural landscape. Different views have different attractions. Here, the clerk of the travel agency should recommend the visiting places according to the guests' interest.

- Departure & arrival time

For group tour, the departure and arrival time is decided by the guests. You should ask the guests when they would like to go and return.

- Transportation

There are three types of transport from overseas to the destination, by cruise ship, by train and by air. City transportation includes buses, taxis, subways, coaches and rent cars. You need to recommend the easiest way to transport.

- Accommodation

The accommodation includes resorts, hotels, motels, inns, bed & breakfasts and hostels. Hotels are generally the most common way. You can also recommend the local accommodations.

- Food & beverages

In general, a group tour includes three meals a day. The food may be team meal, buffet, fast food or local cuisine. Guests may have special needs, such as vegetarians, therefore, the clerk should let the guests choose how to have meals during the tour.

5. Useful sentences.

(1) Greet customers at the travel agency.

◇ For a clerk

- Good morning, ABC travel agency. How can I help you?
- Welcome, sir/madam. How may I help you?
- Welcome to our travel agency. What can I do for you?

◇ For a tourist

- Could you do me a fever?
- Could you give me a hand?
- Good morning, I'd like to have a look at your tour package to Changsha.
- Excuse me, could you recommend a place for me to spend my weekends?

(2) Ask customers' information.

◇ For a clerk

- May I know your name?
- May I know your contact number?
- May I know your email?
- How many people are there in your group/party?
- When would you like to depart?
- When are you planning the tour?
- How long are you going to stay here?
- What kind of tour do you want, group or FIT?
- What tourist sites are you interested in?
- How are you going there, by air or by train?
- Do you need a tour guide?

◇ For a tourist

- My name is Lily, Chou.
- My telephone number is 156-7133-8926.
- My email address is lvyou@citsag.com.
- We have six persons.
- Six in all

- I'd like to depart on Nov. 23 by air.

- We want to stay for about 7 days.

- I'd like to take a group tour.

- I'd like an inclusive tour.

- Do you have an English speaking tour guide?

- How many people will be in this tour?

- How many people will join this tour?

(3) Ask for travel information.

◇ For a clerk

- We have several tour packages here.

- Please have a look at our brochure.

- I'd like to recommend a four-day-three-night tour to you.

- This tour package is daily departure.

- This tour lasts for seven days.

- We can arrange a hotel for you.

- The tour bus will pick you up from the airport and take you to the hotel.

- The tour package includes round-trip high speed railway tickets between Changsha and Beijing, four night's accommodation in Beijing and three meals a day.

- On the first day, the tour group will visit the Great Wall. On the second day, we will go to Tian'anmen Square and the Imperial Palace.

- An English speaking tour guide will be at your service from the beginning to the end.

- May I suggest a 3-day-2-night tour package to you?

- Can you tell me what date would you like to depart?

- When are you planning the travel?

◇ For a tourist

- Can you recommend several good tour packages to South Korea?

- Could you tell me more about this tour package?

- Please recommend some interesting attractions to visit.

- What does the city tour/tour package include?
- May I know your itinerary for this tour?
- How long does the tour last?
- How long does the flight take?
- Does the package include three meals a day?
- Where will we live for the night?
- Could you help us reserve the hotel?
- How many places will we visit?
- Is it possible for us to visit Orange Island?
- Could you send me an email about the details?
- I'd like to book this tour package.

(4) Ask about the price.

◇ For a tourist

- What is the price for this tour package?
- What are included in your charges?
- Can I get a discount?

◇ For a clerk

- The price is US $ 80 per person.
- The charges include the round-trip flight tickets, three night's accommodation, three meals a day and entry to the tourist sites.
- If you take this route, we will offer you 20% discount.
- The price can be lower if there are more people.
- The insurance is included in your package.
- What's your budget for this tour?
- Dose the flight fare include breakfast?

(5) Other.

- Do you have any special requirement?
- Do you mind if I check the details?
- I'd like to go ahead and make a reservation.

- Please fill in the registration form.
- You can book the tour on the Internet.
- You can contact us on telephone or by email.
- You will receive the travel leaflet soon.

Module 2
Receiving Tasks

A good beginning is half the success. Receiving tasks is an important work procedure of tour guide service. After receiving the tasks from the travel agency, the guide should be prepared to receive the guests, which includes being familiar with the reception plan, reconfirming the arrangement and preparing for meeting the tour group. The pre-reception work refers to all kinds of work since the guide accepts the reception plan from the travel agency, which should be double-checked to make sure the whole journey goes well.

◇ Learning Objectives

Knowledge

① Understand the basic content of a reception plan.

② Master the vocabulary, useful expressions and sentences related to pre-reception work.

Skills

① Be able to reconfirm the arrangement.

② Be able to do preparing work according to the reception plan.

Quality

① Improve the ability to make immediate response according to circumstances.

② Take career responsibility of a tour guide.

Task 1　Familiar with the plan

◇Lead-in

Simon is a guide of the China International Travel Service. This day, he receives a reception plan to serve the tour group CITS20161008A which will visit Changsha and Shaoshan from Oct. 8th to Oct. 10th. After receiving the reception plan, Simon is about to prepare the pre-reception work as soon as possible. The reception plan covers too much information. What do you think he should do to process and utilize such information correctly and rapidly?

◇Analyzing the Task

Before the group's arrival, Simon should read the reception plan (see Table 2-1) and tour itinerary (see Table 2-2), and understand the service and requirements of the tour group in detail. What's more, he should record the important matters.

① The main information of the tour group.

According to the reception plan and tour itinerary, the main information of the tour group Simon should pay attention to includes: the travel agency's name and number, the settlement way of the group, the level of the group (e. g. , VIP, deluxe, standard, economic, etc.), the name and telephone number of the contact person, etc.

② The main information of the tourists.

The main information of the tourists contains the tourists' names, gender, occupations and age (to make sure whether there are old people or kids), religions and nationalities.

③ The itinerary and the location of immigration.

Simon should also make the whole route clear, including the transportation, accurate time, the intermediate station(s) and the terminal station, which helps to arrange the schedule and coordinate with the travel agent actively.

④ The transportation.

Simon should grasp the arrival and departure time, the flight (train, ship) number and the airport (station, wharf).

Before going to the next destination, Simon should make sure that the transport has been confirmed as planned, and if there is any change, Simon should reconfirm the ticket. And he also should check whether the airport construction fee is paid by the tourists themselves or by the travel agency. Simon is going to serve the overseas group. He even should find out the flight ticket is the OK ticket or the OPEN ticket. An OK ticket is also called a confirmed ticket, which means a ticket confirms the date, flight and seat. Whereas, an OPEN ticket means a valid ticket for travel that does not specify a date or time, the actual date and time of travel being arranged later.

⑤ Some other special requirements and precautions.

For example, the group asks for personal welcome, banquets or other treatment by related responsible persons.

Table 2-1

The Reception Plan of the Three-Day Tour for Changsha-Shaoshan
No. CITS20161008A

Operation Department, Financial Department,

Organized by the China International Travel Service, 20 people will arrive at Changsha on the date of October 8th, 2016 by Flight CA9525, and they will depart at Changsha on the date of October 10th, 2016 by plane to Hangzhou.

The group will live in Sheraton Changsha reserved by the China International Travel Service with breakfast.

The departure flight tickets are self-service. Please confirm.

Please provide VIP service.

Simon will be the tour guide.

Contact: Micheal   Tel: 13912345678

Attached with the list of Logistics Department.

Copy to the General Manager and the Vice General Manager.

Planned by In-Bound Tour Center

Table 2-2

Itinerary Information

NO. CITS20161008A

Travel Agency	China International Travel Service Guide:Simon Tel:18812345678	
Numbers of Tourists	Male:12 Female:8 Children:2 Total:22	
Accommodation	Star Level:Five-star Rooms:10(Twin-bed:8; Single:2) Total Nights:2	
Catering	Breakfast:Sheraton Changsha Lunch:Changsha Fire Palace Restaurant Dinner:Sheraton Changsha	
Arrival and Departure Time (Number of runs)	Arrive at 4:00 pm, 08/10/2016, by flight CA9525 Depart at 9:00 pm, 10/10/2016, by flight	
Meeting Service	Huanghua International Airport Seeing off Service Huanghua International Airport	
Organizing Travel Agency	China International Travel Service	
Contact	Micheal	Tel:13912345678
National Guide		Tel:
Local Guide		Tel:

续表

	Time	Arrangement	Hotel
Itinerary	08/10/2016	Arrival in Changsha (Enjoy the ethnic customs)	Sheraton Changsha
	09/10/2016	Changsha (Yuelu Academy, Orange Island, the Museum of Hunan Province and the Xiang Embroidery Museum)	Sheraton Changsha
	10/10/2016	Shaoshan (the former residence of Chairman Mao and Statue Square in the morning, the Drop Water Tunnel. Back to Changsha in the afternoon)	

Rental Firm	China Auto Rental	
Driver	Liu Gang	Tel:13512345678
Accompanying Driver		Tel:
License Plate Number	湘A12345	
Notes		

China International Travel Service　　　Operator: Daniel　　　Guide: Simon

◇ Developing Tasks

1. Write down the information according to Table 2-1 and Table 2-2.

① The main information of the tour group.

② The main information of the tourists.

③ The itinerary and the location of immigration.

④ The transportation.

⑤ Some other special requirements and precautions.

2. Phrases interpreting.

带团委托书		单人间	
全陪		中国国际旅行社	
接待计划		入境	
三天两夜		始发站	
标准间		终点站	

3. Listen and fill in the blanks.

Listen to the following passage and fill in the missing words in the blanks.

Welcome to all of you... can everybody see and hear me? Good... I'm Sally, your guide for this tour of the Bicentennial Park... I hope that you're all wearing your most comfortable shoes and that you can ___①___ the pace. So let's get under way on our tour around this wonderful park. I'll start today with some general ___②___. There used to be a lot of factories in this area until the 1960s. Creating the park required demolition of lots of derelict buildings on the site, so most of the exciting park space all around you was originally ___③___. The idea of building a public park here was first discussed when ___④___ proposed a high-rise housing development, but the local community wasn't happy.

If the land was to be cleaned up, they wanted to use the site for ___⑤___. Residents wanted open space for ___⑥___, rather than housing or even an indoor sports complex. Now to the Bicentennial Park itself. It has two areas, a ___⑦___ and a formal park with ___⑧___ and gardens. The tall blue-and-white building in front of us is called The Tower and is the central point for the formal gardens. It stands ___⑨___, so follow me up the stairs to where we can ___⑩___ the fantastic views. Well, here we are at the top of The Tower, and we're going to look at the view from each direction.

Task 2　　Reconfirm the arrangement

◇Lead-in

After reading and understanding the plan, Simon finds there are so many things should be confirmed. In order to make sure everything is alright and provide high-quality service, what arrangement do you think needs to be triple-checked the day before the group's arrival?

◇Analyzing the Task

The service arrangement covers all kinds of work involved in the journey ranging from the touring vehicles, accommodation, restaurants, baggage delivery to the condition of the scenic spots, which all need to be put into practice with the relevant departments or personnel before the group's arrival.

① Reconfirm the transportation.

Simon needs to contact with the car team or car company who provides the transportation service, and then should ask and verify the driver's name, phone number, and the car number. In addition, the car which services large tour groups should be marked with a tag. Tell the specific pick-up point and time to the driver as well as the general itinerary.

② Reconfirm the accommodation.

A guide should be familiar with the name, location, situation, facilities and service of the hotel where the group will stay, such as the distance from the city center, the nearby shopping spots, traffic conditions, etc. Moreover, Simon should check the room numbers, level, time and the room charge with the hotel sales department or the front desk to make sure they correspond to the reception plan. At the same time, he also needs to provide the arrival time to the hotel.

③ Reconfirm the catering.

Contact with the related restaurants in advance, to confirm every meal included in the itinerary. The information covers the date, the group number, the number of the dinners, the standard of food and beverages and special requirements, etc.

④ Reconfirm the luggage handling service.

Travel agencies always provide baggage handling service according to the number of a group, hence Simon should learn about the specific provisions. If the group is equipped with a baggage car, Simon should be aware of the service vehicles and related personnel, and then get in touch with them ahead of time to make them know the arrival time, place and hotel.

⑤ Be familiar with the scenic spots.

If there are some new tourist attractions or unfamiliar scenic spots in the itinerary, Simon should get to know its general situation in order to visit smoothly, such as the opening time, the best tour route, toilet location, etc.

⑥ Contact with the national guide.

If the group is equipped with a national guide, Simon should also contact with the national guide in advance to make sure the time and location for meeting the tourists, and to prevent any missing or omitting accident.

The on-the-spot communication is as following.

(Reconfirm the accommodation)

(A=the receptionist   B=the tour guide)

A: Hello, Jingang Hotel Room Reservation, what can I do for you, please?

B: Hello, I am the guide from Ningbo City Travel Agency, and my name is John. I'm calling to confirm if you received the reservation for the group form Canada.

A: Please wait a moment. I'll check it. Is the group number AFC-TD-090929-2?

B: Yes, you're right.

A: OK, they'll check in tomorrow night, and the number of the people is 10, four double standard rooms, one single room, one king-size room, right?

B: Yes, can you make sure that all the rooms face south with a view on the top floor?

A: Well, we have reserved in accordance with the requirements of your reservation.

B: OK, thank you very much. And for the convenience of the guests, can you try to make the group members live on the same floor?

A: Well, no problem, you don't have too many guests.

B: Thank you for your cooperation, and the group has the Western-style breakfast, isn't it?

A: Well, that's right.

B: The last thing is that the group will check in after five o'clock tomorrow evening. Please inform your bellboy to be well prepared at that time. Thank you very much. Good bye!

A: My pleasure. Good-bye!

◇ Developing Tasks

1. Listen and fill in the blanks.

Listen to the following dialogue and try to fill in the missing words in the blanks.

R: Beijing Hotel. Reservation desk. Can I help you?

G: I'm calling from New York. I'd like to reserve a room in your hotel.

R: What kind of room would you like, sir? We have single rooms, double rooms, suites and ___①___ suites.

G: I'd like to book a double room from October 1 to October 7.

R: Would you like breakfast?

G: No, thanks.

R: Hold on please. I'll check if there is a room ___②___ for those days.

G: OK.

R: Sorry to have kept you waiting, sir. We'll have rooms available in that ___③___.

G: How much do you ___④___ for a double room?

R: The ___⑤___ rate is $120 per night.

G: OK. I'll take it. By the way, I'd like to have a quiet room if ___⑥___.

R: A quiet room is ___⑦___. Could you give me your name, please?

G: George Smith. S-M-I-T-H.

R: Thank you, Mr. Smith. And what time will you be arriving, Mr. Smith?

G: Around 6:00 p.m. Do you have a ___⑧___ service?

R: We have an airport ___⑨___ to receive our guests there.

G: Oh, that's good.

R: Well, Mr. Smith. A double room without breakfast from October 1 to October 7. Am I right, Mr. Smith?

G: Yes, thank you.

R: Thank you for calling, Mr. Smith. You'll be ___⑩___ to be here then. Good-bye.

2. Complete the following dialogue and then play the roles in pairs.

A：Hello. Who is that?

B：Hello, is that Mr. Ma? _____①_____

（我是中国国际旅行社的导游 Mary）

A：Yes, where shall we meet tomorrow?

B：_____②_____

（麻烦您明天下午4点准时到北京机场接来自澳大利亚的10位客人，可以吗？）

A：Well, that's good.

B：By the way, is your license plate number Zhejiang B20233?

A：Yes, it's a blue 17-seat Jinlong bus.

B：_____③_____

（我想确认一下车上的麦克风和空调都还好吧？）

A：No problem.

B：That's great. I'll give you a brief introduction of the itinerary, _____④_____

（他们将在北京进行为期5天的参观旅游，明天下午4点从北京机场出发，入住北京国际饭店后稍做休息，晚上6点半去吃晚饭，请问您有什么问题吗？）

A：That's alright with me, so will they live in Beijing for five nights?

B：No, they will live in Beijing International Hotel for four nights. I will tell you the details later.

A：All right.

B：Then see you tomorrow!

A：OK, bye.

3. Simulation.

Guide Xiao Li calls to reconfirm the catering in Walton Hotel. Make a dialogue based on the situation given below：

① Time：16:00 on September 29, 2017

② Location：Walton Hotel

③ The number of people：9 adults and 1 child

④ Requirements：One of the guest is a vegetarian; food should be a little spicy, but not too salty.

Task 3 Preparations for meeting a tour group

Lead-in

Reconfirming the arrangement is an important part of the preparation for meeting a tour group. After contacting with the related departments, Simon turns to prepare some necessary materials.

Analyzing the Task

Before meeting the tourists, Simon should prepare:

① Some necessary materials, such as the reception plan, guide ID card, name tag, guide flag, pick-up board, settlement documents, notebook and some other items.

② Some corresponding knowledge, for example, knowledge of leading a group, knowledge of the new sightseeing spots or special sightseeing spots, at the same time, he also need to keep an eye on some current topics, major news at home and abroad, or some other topics visitors may be of interest.

③ Personal images. Simon's dress / attire should be in step with the local dress habits and the nationality as well as the identity of a tour guide.

④ The psychological preparation, which mainly includes two aspects.

First, Simon should be ready to face complex and hard work.

Second, due to the complexity of the tourists, sometimes the guide will accept complaints and nagging even though he or she has done everything to provide warm and thoughtful service for the tour group.

Developing Tasks

1. Match each picture below with the words or phrases.

① ② ③

④　　　　　　　⑤　　　　　　⑥

a. tour-guiding flags　　b. pick-up board　　c. loud-speaker

d. backpack　　e. guide ID card　　f. first aid kit

2. Discussion.

Discuss the following situation in groups and find out the reason. Then give some solutions.

Miss Sue is a tour guide from China Travel Service who is young and beautiful. From a well-off family, Miss Sue is good-dressed and fashionable. Once Miss Sue received a foreign tour group whose members were young ladies around 30 years old. When Miss Sue appeared, these young ladies were overshadowed by her. And during the visit, Miss Sue always changed her costumes of famous brands, which made the young lades as a foil to her in the group. Therefore, in the process of visit, although Miss Sue provided courteous service, the young ladies didn't want to be together with her. Miss Sue had a feeling of being slighted.

3. Translation.

Translate the following passage into Chinese.

Cultural practices, cultural differences, local manners, and mores: traveling can be a behavioral minefield, even when you have the best intentions. Everything from greeting to eating can be an opportunity to do the wrong thing, and not only embarrass yourself, but offend your host countrymen. Once you are on the ground of a different country, remain highly sensitive to native behavior. Never be completely surprised by anything; try to take it in stride, and don't feel offended if something seems offensive—like queue jumping. After all, this is a global village, and we are all very different.

4. What places of interest are there in Hunan Province? Please write down.

◇ Related Knowledge

1. Talking about the reception task.

A: Hi, Sunny speaking.

B: Hello, Sunny. There is a reception task for you.

A: When? / For which days?

B: From March 8 to 10, 3 days & 2 nights.

A: How many visitors are there in the party?

B: 18 adults, no kids.

A: Where are the visitors from?

B: England.

A: How about the quality grade?

B: Luxurious.

A: It sounds wonderful. Where is the destination?

B: Changsha-ShaoShan.

A: OK, no problem. I'll take it.

B: Thank you and good luck.

2. The work procedures of a tour guide—preparations.

You start your work as soon as you get the reception program from the travel agency. The program usually contains the code of the tourist group, the names of the tour members, the time for arrival and departure, the types of transportation, and the sightseeing schedule, etc.

(1) Read the program.

You should read the program carefully, and get information from the program mentioned above. You should pay more attention to these: who pays the airport construction fee, your company or the tourists themselves? Which airport are you going to meet your group?

(2) Research on the tourists.

You should make careful research on the tourists so that you can get well prepared. For example, for a group of doctors, you should prepare for topics on medicine, such as the acupuncture anesthesia or Chinese herb medicine. For a group of housewives, your topics may be about women in China, and Chinese cooking and you should leave them more time for shopping.

You should also see if there is a vegetarian or someone who avoids eating certain food in the group; and anyone who has other purpose except sightseeing, maybe visiting relatives or friends. If this is the case, you may arrange for them in advance. It is also your duty to see if there are old or disabled people in the group. They should be given special care.

(3) Make a reservation in the hotel.

You should book the hotel which meets the standard of the group's request, or the one that the group assigned. Get to know it well: the location of the hotel, the telephone number, and the facilities.

(4) Book the coach.

You should arrange a meeting with the coach driver, from whom you can find out: the type of the coach, how many people it can take, and the number and color of the coach. You should also know the name of the driver, his driving experience and fix the time and place to meet again.

(5) Arrange meals.

You should make reservations in the restaurants. Tell the restaurants the actual time for meals, the number of people for dining, the special requirements for food, and the way of payments.

(6) Confirm the plane, train or ship.

You should telephone the airport, the railway station or the harbor to confirm ETA (the Estimated Time of Arrival) in case there is any change.

(7) Contact the travel agency that is in charge of the tour program in the next stop.

In order to make the tour go smoothly, you should contact the travel agency that is responsible for the tour in the next stop in advance. Make sure that the agency has confirmed your fax and has everything well organized.

(8) Collect pamphlets and get things needed ready.

You should prepare pamphlets, tourist maps, introductions of scenic spots and places for visit. Things needed are admission tickets to the sightseeing spots, a megaphone, small flags, medicine and rain protections.

3. Useful sentences.

(1) Reconfirm the accommodation.

◇ We've booked a twin-bed room with a bath three weeks ago for Mr. Grimes.

◇ A double room with a front view is 140 dollars per night; one with a rear view is 115 dollars per night.

◇ I think I'll take the one with a front view then.

◇ What services come with that rate?

◇ By the way, I'd like a quiet room away from the street if that is possible.

(2) Reconfirm the catering.

◇ You can sign for your meals and drinks in the restaurants and the bars in the hotel by showing your keys.

◇ There are ten people who have completely vegetarian diet. Please cook more bamboo shoots, fungi and soy products and vegetables food.

◇ Please get the ice-cold beer and drinks in advance.

◇ Please do not put pepper into the dishes and don't be too salty; light diet would be better.

◇ The group is expected to be arrived at 6:30 in the evening; please get ready. And please leave a great parking space at the gate.

(3) Reconfirm the itinerary.

◇ The itinerary covers so many places.

◇ I'm sure the coastal sunshine and mild wind from the sea will make the seaside tour one of the most unforgettable experiences in your life.

◇ By the way, I shall appreciate it very much if you would fit in whatever you can.

◇ I absolutely agree with you about the itinerary.

◇ The change on the itinerary will surely make it more practical and, therefore, more satisfactory.

◇ Thank you very much for such a full and interesting itinerary.

◇ We would be very pleased if you could give us more details of the international events held annually in Nanning.

◇ I hope everybody in this group will be physically fit for this long trip.

Module 3
Immigration and Customs

Assisting tourists to go through immigration and customs at the destination airport is extremely important for a smooth journey. In the process of entering an foreign country, the tour leader should conduct a good service in the following tasks: help the tour group to check in at the airport, check in luggage, complete immigration formalities, claim luggage, go through customs clearance.

As the tourists might have trouble with the check-in, customs formalities, luggage declaration, the tour leaders should help with each procedure to speed up the process. Careful and experienced service is most expected.

◇ Learning Objectives

Knowledge

① Know the work process about checking in, going through immigration and customs.

② Master the vocabulary and expressions about check-in, immigration and customs.

Skills

① Be able to check in for a tour group.

② Be able to answer questions from customs officers.

③ Be able to fill out the arrival card and the declaration card.

④ Be able to give necessary reminders about customs requirements.

Quality

① Enhance service efficiency and accuracy.

② Foster self-study ability, problem-solving ability and communication ability.

Task 1　Check in at the airport

◇**Lead-in**

Sally is a tour leader from TITI TRAVEL in UK. Her present task is in responsible of leading the tour group CITS20161008A which is going to leave London to Changsha (Hunan, China) on Oct. 8th. As planned, the tour members are gathered at Heathrow Airport around 10 a.m. to take the flight BA039 at 12:30 p.m. To ensure that every tourist can board on time, how should Sally check in for the group?

◇**Analyzing the Task**

Sally can properly check in for the tour group as following.

① Checking in for the tour members and meet their needs.

Before checking in, Sally should ask the tourists' preference about seats or any special requirements. Then checking the flight details and counting the number of the tourists are important when checking in at the counter.

Some tourists of this tour group want to take a window seat. Besides, there are three vegetarians in the group and they prefer vegetarian meals during the flight. So a key task of check-in is to meet every member's demand.

② Checking in for tourists' luggage.

Sally should tell the tour members about the airline's requirement on weight and size of checked luggage in advance.

But still several tourists of the group might take a luggage that excesses the free allowance. In such a situation, asking the tourists to deal with the excess weight is expected.

③ Communicating with the airline clerk at the check-in counter in a clear and professional manner.

The on-the-spot communication is as following:

(C=the clerk of the check-in counter   S=Sally)

C: Good morning, madam. What can I do for you?

S: Excuse me, is this the counter for HM 268 to China?

C: Yes, madam. Are you from the same group?

S: Yes, we are.

C: Please go to the next counter for group check-in.

* * * * * * * * * * * * * * * * * * * *

S: Hello Miss, we are a group of 35 people going to China by flight HM 268.

C: May I see your passports and tickets, please?

S: Sure, here you are.

C: How many pieces of luggage would you like to check in?

S: Forty pieces altogether.

C: Please put them on scale... Oh, I'm sorry that our free allowance is 35 kilograms, but these three suitcases excess the weight.

S: In that case, how much should we pay for the overweight respectively?

C: Let me count... Clearly, we have to charge you 50 dollars for this one that excesses 5 kilo, 60 dollars for that one that excesses 6 kilos and 30 dollars for the baggage that is only 3 kilos overweight.

S: Okay, I'll ask the three members whether they would like to reduce the weight or pay for it.

C: Sure, I'll check in for the rest. Is there any special request about seats?

S: Yes, Ms. Smith and Ms. Clark would like a window seat. By the way, three members said that they have ordered vegetarian meals at your web. Could you please check it?

C: Sure, now I'm going to check in for these 35 passengers one by one. Please wait for a while.

S: Thanks a lot.

◇ Developing Tasks

1. Please write down the language in each corresponding task.

Tasks	Language
Explain to the tourists whose luggage is overweight. Tell them clearly how the airline charges for excess weight.	
Tell the counter clerk that the tourists' special request.	
Check the board gate and the flying time with the clerk.	
After checking in, ask the tourists to receive their passports.	

2. Simulation.

Sally is checking in for the tour group at the counter, but one of the tour members feels uncomfortable and would like to change to a first-class ticket. Please make a dialogue with a clerk and specially ask him/her how a passenger could up-grade a class.

3. Fill in the blanks with the right words according to the recording.

Online Check-in

Online check-in is the process in which passengers ① their presence on a flight through the Internet and print their own ② . Depending on the specific flight, passengers may also enter details such as ③ options and ④ quantities and select their preferred ⑤ .

 ## Task 2　Go through the immigration

◇ Lead-in

The tour group CITS20161008A has arrived at Huanghua International Airport in Changsha on August 10th. As a tour leader, how could Sally assist the members to go through the immigration?

◇ Analyzing the Task

Sally can properly lead the tour group to enter China with the following tasks:

① Giving required certificates and documents to immigration inspectors.

The required certificates for immigration are passports, visas, flight tickets and arriving cards. Since the tour group has got a group visa, the members should follow the directions of the officer at the immigration station and go through the formalities at the assigned counter. Sally should walk in the front of the group, handing the tour visa to the immigration officer and preparing to answer his or her questions.

② Answering questions.

Sally needs to answer the questions from the customs officer. These questions usually include: a. What's the purpose of visiting the country? b. How many people are there in the group? c. How long do you plan to stay in the country? d. How many places do you plan to visit in the country? e. Where do you live during your stay here? f. How much money do you take with you? g. What's the native travel agent in responsible for reception?

③ Claiming checked luggage.

Before leading the tour members to go through the next formalities, Sally should make sure that every member has claimed their checked luggage.

④ Communicating with the immigration officer in a clear and professional manner.

The on-the-spot communication is as following.

(O=the immigration officer   S=the tour leader)

O: Good morning, Madam. May I have your passport and arrival card, please?

S: I'm the leader of the tour group and we have a group visa.

O: Please show me all the members' passports and your group visa.

S: Sure, here you are.

O: I'm going to check it. What's the purpose of your visit in Changsha?

S: We come here for please and we are going to visit some places.

O: How long will you stay in China?

S: We'll leave on May 25th, so it would be 5 days together.

O: Do you have a return ticket?

S: Yes, here you are.

O: Where do you intend to stay during the time here?

S: In the hotels. Here are the booking confirmation letters.

O: Okay, there is no problem with your visa and passports. Please let your members keep their arrival cards in their passports. Then let them go through one by one according to the order of the name list.

S: Thanks a lot.

◇ **Developing Tasks**

1. Please fill the arrival card.

One of the tour leader's tasks is to help the members of the group to fill in the arrival cards when they arrive at the destination.

FULL NAME (AS APPEARS IN PASSPORT):
PASSPORT NO.:
DATE OF EXPIRY(DD-MM-YYYY): SEX: MALE　FEMALE
PLACE OF ISSUE:
NATIONALITY:
CITY OF RESIDENCE:
COUNTRY OF RESIDENCE:
LAST PLACE OF EMBARKATION:
FLIGHT NO.:

2. Listen to a flight announcement and fill in the blanks.

Ladies and gentlemen, ①_____ please. Because of ②_____ old weather, we have to wait for snow ③_____ , our flight will be ④_____ for about an hour. Now we will ⑤_____ beverages/dinner/snack. We will ⑥_____ you of further details as soon as possible. Thanks for your understanding and ⑦_____ .

3. Fill in the blanks with the words given below.

prohibit　tax　smuggler　item　non-smoking　dutiable

① _____ goods were found in the suitcase of the suspicious man.

② The policeman caught the _____ at the airport when he tried to go through immigration.

③ Customers are not allowed to smoke in the _____ section at the restaurant.

④ The duty-free _____ include several personal belongings.

⑤ It is required to declare _____ objects at the customs.

⑥ You have to pay _____ on some imported goods according to the regulation.

Task 3 Go through the customs

Lead-in

After immigration inspection, all members of the tour group CITS20161008A have to go through customs formalities. One of the important procedures is to declare articles to the customs. How could Sally explain the declaration requirements to the members and assist them to go through customs formalities?

Analyzing the Task

Sally can properly lead the tour group go through the customs with the following tasks.

① Assisting the tour members to go through customs inspection.

There are four kinds of inspection ways at the customs: a. exemption; b. oral declaration; c. filling out the declaration form with seldom open-case inspection; d. filling out the declaration form with open-case inspection. In this case, Sally should clearly tell the tour members what articles are required to declare and how to fill out the declaration form.

② Leading the tour members to go through customs.

Customs inspection is generally a routine spot check. After handing the declaration forms to the officer, the tour leader could lead the tour group to walk through the customs directly. But the officer has a right to make a pat-down search on a tourist directly as a spot check. So in case of unnecessary dispute, Sally should warn the members that they need to cooperate with the officer if he would like to make a spot check.

③ Explanation of declaration requirements.

The explanation is as follows.

Well, it's great that we've all gone through the Immigration Office smoothly. Now I have something important to tell you; please pay attention to it. According to the regulation of Custom Inspection in China, you have to declare some goods at the customs, such articles including electric equipment, foreign currency, jewelry, gold, silver, antiques and other treasure. So if you have taken any of those articles in your luggage, please put a check mark on the customs declaration form and give it to the officer when you go through the customs. During the enquiry, you have to report immediately, correctly and frankly the details of your items. Now I'm going to hand out the declaration form to everyone. Please ask me without hesitation if you have any questions. Thanks!

◇ **Developing Tasks**

1. Listen to the paragraph and fill in the blanks.

Visa

Visa is an official mark put on a passport by representatives of the ____①____ country. It gives holders permission to enter, pass through or leave a ____②____ country. There are different types of visa according to the ____③____ of visiting the country, including: on education, on ____④____, for traveling, for ____⑤____, for visiting relatives, etc.

2. Make dialogue with your partner according to the following situation.

You are a tourist visiting China. Your partner is a customs officer. There is a parcel of British spice. The customs officer asks you to open the parcel to check what is in it.

3. Translation from Chinese to English.

① 我给朋友带了些小礼物，另外还在飞机上买了一瓶香水。

② 请在离开海关前吃完这些进口水果，否则我们将要没收它们。

③ 如果你有东西需要申报，请填好申报表并走红色通道。

④ 美国海关规定，十美元以下的礼品可以免税带出。

⑤ 海关有时会让你登记一下随身携带的外汇。

◇ **Related Knowledge**

1. How to check in at the airport.

① Hand in required documents for check-in.

② Check information about flight and destination.

③ Check in for luggage.

④ Get a boarding pass.

2. Top tips for speeding your way through the customs.

No matter whether your overseas adventure is about to start or draws to a close, you will be asked to fill out a customs declaration form, the first step in completing your Customs and Border Protection passport inspection.

When you arrive at an international border, a Customs and Border Protection officer will review your declaration form, examine your passport and ask you about your trip and about the items you are bringing with you.

If you plan ahead, you can help make the customs inspection process flow smoothly. Here are some top tips for quickly clearing customs.

Keep Your Packing List

The first step in determining which items to declare is to make a list of all the things you brought with you from home. This packing list will not only help you organize your suitcase at the beginning of your trip, it will also assist you when the time to fill out your customs declaration form arrives.

Know the Rules

Each country has different customs regulations. Take time to read these rules before your trip begins so that you know which items you cannot bring back. The governments of the United States, Canada and the United Kingdom, for example, all provide customs information for travelers on their websites.

Register Valuable Items

You can register high-value items, such as cameras, laptop computers and watches, with your country's customs agency before you travel. Taking this step will help provide Customs and Border Protection officers with proof of ownership of these items and save you time and trouble when you return home.

Save Receipts

Bring an envelope or zip-top plastic bag with you for receipt storage. Any time you buy something during your travels, tuck the receipt into your envelope or bag. When the time comes for you to fill out your customs declaration form, you will have a handy record of your purchases.

Avoid Farms and Agricultural Stations While Traveling

Customs officers are charged with preventing agricultural pests from entering the country. Any traveler who has visited a farm or agricultural station may be subject to additional screening, disinfection of shoes and other precautionary measures. If possible, skip the goat farm tour and save yourself time and trouble when you go through customs.

Leave Food Items Behind

Trying new foods is part of the fun of international travel. However, many countries restrict imports of fruits, vegetables and meat products. Eat the food you bought on your trip before you head to the airport.

Pack Carefully for Your Return Trip

If possible, pack all the items you purchased on your trip in just one or two places. This will make it easy for you to find them if the customs officer asks to see them. Of course, you should never place valuable items in your checked baggage. Instead, pack them in your carry-on bag so that you can keep them with you at all times.

The Bottom Line

While going through customs is an unavoidable process, there are things you can do to minimize the time you spend with the customs officer. Going through customs will not be painful, provided you plan ahead and prepare for your customs interview.

Module 4
Meeting Guests

    Meeting tourists is the first direct contact between guides and tourists, which is vital throughout the whole reception process in tourism. Well begun is half done. In the very beginning of the reception service, tour guides must show their hospitality and consideration to the tourists, cherish all the time to communicate with the tourists, because they will stay with the tourists only for several days.

    Generally speaking, the process of meeting guests at the airport includes confirming the arrival time, contacting with the driver, standing at a highly visible location with a flag and a welcome board, finding the guests, greeting the guests, checking nationality, group code, number of the tourists and name of the tour leader, counting the luggage and leading the guests to the coach.

◇ Learning Objectives

Knowledge

① Know the work process about meeting guests at the airport.

② Master the vocabulary and expressions about meeting guests.

Skills

① Be able to identify the right guests in time and give warm welcome.

② Be able to check the related information of the guests.

③ Be able to count the number of the tourists and luggage quickly.

④ Be able to help the guests get on the tour bus.

Quality

① Strengthen service consciousness and confidence.

② Foster problem-solving ability and interpersonal communication ability.

Task 1　Meet the tour group

◇Lead-in

Simon, a local guide from CITS, is waiting for the tour group CITS20161008A from England, with a flag and a welcome board in his hands. There are 20 members, and the tour leader is John Smith. The plane has arrived and the passengers are just coming out. What should Simon do at this moment?

◇Analyzing the Task

Simon must do as following.

① Look for the tourists or tour group and the tour leader at a striking position at the station exit, and confirm the information of the tourist group to ensure receiving the right group.

② Greet and self-introduce.

③ Confirm the number of the tourists and luggage.

④ Congregate and lead the guests to the tour bus.

⑤ Help the tourists to get on the bus: stand by the bus door with smile, help the old and the young, and make sure everyone is here.

⑥ Head for the hotel.

The on-the-spot communication is as following.

(S: Simon　　J: John Smith　　T: the tourists　　D: the driver)

S: Excuse me, I'm looking for a tour group from England. Are you the tourists from TITICACA Travel?

T: Yes.

S: Who is the tour leader, please?

T: The man behind with a plaid shirt is the tour leader.

S: Thank you, please wait a minute. I go to meet the leader. (Simon walks to the leader) Excuse me, are you Mr. John Smith from England TITICACA Travel?

J: Yes, I am.

S: And is this your tour group code?

J: Er, let me see, oh yes.

S: Glad to meet you, Mr. Smith. I'm Simon, your local guide from Hunan China International Travel Service.

J: Oh, nice to meet you, Simon.

S: Shall we go there? It's more quiet.

J: OK. (Everybody, follow me please.)

S: Welcome to Changsha.

J: We're so glad you've come to meet us at the airport, Simon.

S: My pleasure. Did you have a nice trip?

J: Yes, it's quite pleasant. But we feel a bit tired after the long flight.

S: Yes, you must. You all need a good rest first. Is everyone in the group here?

J: Yes, a party of twenty five.

S: You added 2 guests?

J: Yes.

S: Are they men or women? Do they need separate rooms?

J: No, they are a couple; one room is fine.

S: (Simon counts the number in her mind) Yes, twenty-five. And how many pieces of luggage do you have?

J: Twenty-five, and we have got them.

S: Good, shall we go to the bus now?

J: Sure.

S: Fine, I'd like to say hello to the group. (Simon faces the group and waves his hands) Hello, I'm your local guide, Simon. Welcome to China! Welcome to Changsha! Now please follow me, ladies and gentleman. Our bus is just waiting in the parking lot. Don't get lost.

J: That's fine. Hurry up, guys!

S: This way, please.

S: (Simon leads them to the bus.) Here we are, ladies and gentlemen. This is our driver, Mr. Wang.

D: Nice to meet you!

S: Mr. Wang is going to help us to put our luggage in the trunk.

J: Well, ladies and gentlemen, look, our coach has a big belly here. Put in your luggage, please. Then get on the coach and find yourself a comfortable seat.

(Then Simon stands by the bus and helps the group get on the bus. After they get on the bus, Simon counts the number in her mind to make sure everyone is on the bus. And then they head for the hotel.)

◇ Developing Tasks

1. Match each picture below with the words or phrases.

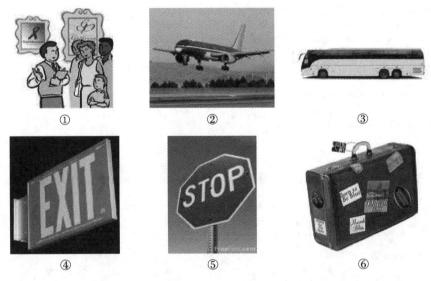

① ② ③

④ ⑤ ⑥

a. coach   b. tour guide   c. exit   d. baggage   e. sign   f. flight

2. Interpret the phrases.

问询处		一行25人	
导游证		机场班车	
导游旗		行李箱	
接站牌		领队	
地陪		走失	

3. Discuss and write.

① If you are a local guide, what should you do to fully prepare for the task of receiving a tour group?

_____

_____

_____

_____

_____

② What can you do to make yourself easily visible to your guests at the airport or at the railway station?

_____

_____

_____

_____

_____

4. Listen and fill in the blanks.

(A=the guide   B=the tour leader   C=the stranger)

A: Excuse me, Madam, ① _____?

C: No, I am not. I'm afraid you've made a mistake.

A: ② _____.

C: That's all right.

A: ③ _____?

B: Yes, I am.

A: ④ _____.
How do you do, Miss Smith?

B: How do you do, Miss Lin? Thank you for meeting us.

A: I'm glad to be of service, Miss Smith. Welcome to Fuzhou. ⑤ _____?

B: I'm sorry to say one man didn't come for business reasons. We now have 21 people including me.

A: That's all right. However, ⑥_____.

B: Sorry to cause you trouble.

A: No trouble. Now, ⑦_____?

B: Of course. Here you are. There are 16 pieces altogether. Will we have our luggage once we reach the hotel?

A: ⑧_____.

B: I'm glad to hear that. Shall we go now?

A: Yes, of course. ⑨_____.

B: Sure. You ⑩_____ and we'll follow.

5. Simulation.

Sunny, the local guide from CITS, is receiving Sunshine Tour Group of 26 members from Canada at Fuzhou Changle International Airport. The tour leader is James Brown. The arrival time is 9 a.m. She will accompany them to the West Lake Hotel.

Task 2　Meet a FIT guest

◇Lead-in

At the airport, Simon, a local guide from CITS, is waiting for an individual traveler, Mr. Robert. There comes an American. What should Simon do at this moment?

◇Analyzing the Task

Simon should approach the guest immediately.

The on-the-spot communication is as following.

(S: Simon　　　R: David Robert)

S: Excuse me, are you Mr. David Robert?

D: Yes, I am.

S: Nice to meet you, Mr. Robert. I'm Simon, your local guide from Hunan China International Travel Service.

D: Oh, nice to meet you, Simon. Thank you for coming to meet me.

S: My pleasure. And welcome to Hunan. Did you enjoy your flight, Mr. Robert?

D: Yes, it's quite nice. I managed to sleep part of the way, but I feel a bit tired after a 13-hour flight.

S: Not too tired I hope. The shuttle bus is waiting outside. Shall we go to the hotel now?

D: Good idea.

S: Come this way, please. May I help you with your suitcase?

D: Thank you Simon. It's very kind of you.

◇ Developing Tasks

1. Discuss and write down.

What travel agencies do you know? Please write down at least 5 travel agencies' names.

_____

_____

_____

_____

2. Discuss and make a dialogue.

When you meet with a foreign guest for the first time, how to chat with her/him? Try to make a dialogue about chatting with an unfamiliar guest.

_____

_____

_____

_____

3. Look at the photos showing meeting tasks. Then fill in the blanks with verbs to complete the description of the tasks.

① _____ the exact arrival time before setting out to the airport.

续表

	Remember the bus number and the driver's name. ____②____ with the driver to fix the meeting time and place.
	____③____ the necessities with you, like the tour guide card, the tour flag, the welcome board, etc.
	____④____ to arrive at the airport 30 minutes ahead of the guests' expected arrival time.
	Wait for the guests: ____⑤____ at a visible location in the lobby, with the tour flag and the welcome board.
	____⑥____ the tour group, greet and self-introduce, and confirm relevant information.
	After ____⑦____ the number of the guests, remind the guests of carrying their personal belongings, and ____⑧____ the group to the coach.

续表

	⑨_____ the number of luggage with the guests and the tour leader, and hand over the luggage to the driver.
	⑩_____ for the hotel when making sure everyone is on the bus.

4. Listen and fill in the blanks.

(A: Lucy   B: Mr. Smith)

A: Good evening, sir. Are you Mr. Smith from England?

B: Ah, yes, ①_____.

A: Glad to meet you, Mr. Smith. ②_____. My name is Lucy. Welcome to China.

B: Hello, I was just ③_____ the guide.

A: ④_____, sir. Would you please ⑤_____ please? The coach is waiting outside. ⑥_____?

B: ⑦_____. But I've made too many flights these days. I could hardly remember how many take-offs and landings I've been through these two days.

A: So, we must ⑧_____ as soon as possible. I've already made a reservation for you.

B: Wonderful. I'm ⑨_____ take a shower as soon as possible.

A: I hope to see you refreshed and revitalized tomorrow morning, as we are going to visit the Great Wall.

B: I'sure I will. Actually, we are ⑩_____ seeing the great wonder in the world.

5. Simulation.

Mary, the local guide from Shan'xi OCTS, is holding an identifying cardboard sign at the arrival lobby of the Xi'an International Airport. Mr. & Mrs. Winston Hill are from the United States. Mrs. Hill is at the baggage claim area, while Mr. Hill comes to contact the guide. Later on they join together and go to the coach waiting in the underground parking lot.

◇ **Related Knowledge**

1. The qualifications for being a good tour guide.

The tour guide is the representative of a travel service. The way in which you carry out your duties has an enormous impact on the functioning of the tour. The impression the tour members will have both of the travel service and China will be based on the professionalism of you. A travel service attaches great importance to the quality of a tour guide.

To be an efficient tour guide, you are required to have facility of the two PQ factors—the professional qualifications and personal qualities. These two factors play a very important role in performing a good job in different customer-contact situations.

The professional qualifications consist of three aspects which are called ASK. ASK here stands for ATTITUDE, SKILLS, and KNOWLEDGE.

2. A full preparation for meeting tourists.

Meeting tourists is the first step of the work of a tour guide. Well begun is half done. To guide a tour group successfully, a guide must try to create a good first impression on his/her tourists. Therefore, you must make a full preparation beforehand. You should be prepared to work in a friendly, gracious, and sincere manner and handle problems enthusiastically and efficiently. Meanwhile, you must be mentally ready to face complaints from the tourists.

With proficient skills and a good command of knowledge, a guide must try to move tourists with a pleasant personality. You are expected to have a high sense of responsibility and be effective, humorous and thoughtful. Also, you must be able to coordinate well with the tourists, their escort/national guide, the coach driver, hotel staff, restaurant receptionists, and all those people concerned.

Once mentally ready, a guide must make some physical preparations as well. Here are some important tips for your reference.

(1) Get the basic information of the group as follows.

The name of the travel agency that organizes the group;

The name of the liaison in charge of the group and his/her telephone number;

The group code;

The name of the tour leader and the national guide;

The number of the tourists;

The names of all the tour members and their nationalities, gender, occupations, ages, religions, and special requests, etc.

(2) Study the itinerary carefully.

Confirm details of transportation, hotels, rooms, restaurants, and meals. Also, arrange luggage delivery if necessary.

Contact the porter and inform him of the destination of the luggage.

Contact the coach driver and go with the coach to the arrival point of the tourists. Sometimes, you and the driver may like to go the airport/railway station separately. This is not unacceptable. However, remember you both should arrive at the airport or railway station at least 30 minutes before the expected arrival time.

After confirming the exact parking place of the coach in the parking lot, you should reconfirm the exact arrival time and stand at a highly visible location in the arrival lobby, in full view of the arriving tourists, with an identifying cardboard.

(3) Bring all the necessary items, including one's tour guide certificate, professional badge, and the itinerary of the group/local travel schedule. Don't forget to bring a tour guide banner or an identifying cardboard sign.

Upon the arrival of the tourists, check the nationality, the group code, the number of the tourists and the name of the tour leader / national guide. Check that all luggage has been claimed and collected by the porter for transfer to the coach. Lead the tour group to the coach and assist with boarding. You should stand by the door to politely greet the tourists and confirm the number in the group.

Some limousines have spacious trunks and the group's luggage travels with its owners. In this case, you are expected to give a hand to those who are in need of help while they're transferring their luggage to the coach or into the coach's trunk.

(4) Keep company with the tourists as closely as possible when you move out to the parking lot. However, sometimes, at some railway stations it's so crowded that your tourists might be unable to follow you closely. Tell them about the coach, its number and location, or its color, etc., just in case some people get off track.

(5) Prepare a welcome speech before meeting the guests. The speech should be brief but full in content.

(6) Dress properly and neatly. Professional uniforms are always highly recommended. However, leisure wear is also considered appropriate and friendly. But remember, a male guide should never wear shorts, a sleeveless shirt, or sandals with socks. A female guide must not wear a mini skirt and her make-up should not be

excessively done.

3. How to meet the foreign tourists at the airport.

The process of meeting guests at the airport includes two stages.

Stage 1　Prior to the guests' arrival

① Confirm the expected arrival time of the flight.

② Arrive at the airport 30 minutes prior to the expected arrival time. Do not let the guests wait for you. And confirm the exact parking place of the coach.

③ Reconfirm the exact arrival time.

④ Contacting with the driver to fix the exact parking place of the coach.

⑤ Stand at a highly visible location at the station exit, in full view of the arriving tourists with a welcome board and a tour flag.

Stag 2　Upon the arrival of the tour group

① Find the guests.

② Give greetings.

③ Give self-introduction.

④ Confirm the nationality, the group code, the number of the tourists and the name of the tour leader.

⑤ Make sure all luggage has been claimed and collected by the porter to transfer to the coach.

⑥ Lead the tour group to the coach and help them to get on the bus.

⑦ Head for the hotel after confirming the number of the group on the bus.

4. The luggage lost.

First: Try your best to look for the luggage and register the loss for the tourist though you are not responsible for the loss.

Second: Take the owner to register the lost property in the lost and found office. With his ticket and luggage tag in hand, he can specify the number for further contact.

Third: Write down the address and the phone number of the airline office. In this way, the owner can keep contact with the people concerned for any further information during the travel. The owner could buy some daily necessities and submit receipts for reimbursement later.

Finally: If the owner still cannot find the luggage before he leaves, you should help the tourist to lodge a claim against the airline company, meanwhile inform the administrative staff of the next stop about the address and the phone number of the airline company so that they can continue to keep in touch.

5. Customs for greeting people.

Shaking hands is a universal way of greeting when people meet for the first time. However, different nations have different rituals. Some normally acceptable rules of etiquette may be considered inappropriate or even impolite on some occasions.

Japanese bow to each other to say "hello" and people in Thailand press their palms together to say that they are happy to meet you. Shaking hands is only popular among officials, scholars, and intellectuals in Thailand and a young woman is never allowed to be seen shaking hands with a man.

Europeans are usually seen kissing cheeks when meeting each other. For example, the French kiss people twice when they meet together; the Dutch even more, they kiss three times! Americans also kiss one or both cheeks, but only when meeting very good friends. Two men do not kiss cheeks.

Hugging makes people feel close. But in Britain, it's regarded as a joke when a man hugs another man. Furthermore, an adult man kissing a British young boy will make the boy embarrassed.

6. Useful sentences.

(1) Finding guests.

◇ Excuse me, sir? Are you Mr. Andy Brown from Britain?

◇ Excuse me, I'm looking for a tour group from the U. S. The leader's name is Maria Carrey.

◇ Good morning, sir, I'm the guide to meet a guest from South Africa. Are you Dr. Victor Hugo?

◇ Are you the tour leader of the group of twenty-five?

◇ Excuse me, aren't you Mr. John Smith from England?

(2) Self-introduction.

◇ I'm a guide from China Youth Travel Service. My name is...

◇ I'm Lin, your local guide from CITS.

◇ I'm your guide in Fuzhou, and my name is...

(3) Giving greetings & responses.

◇ Good morning, Mr. and Mrs. Smith. Welcome to Shanghai.

◇ Good morning, Mr. Chen. Thank you for meeting us here.

◇ How was your trip? / Did you enjoy your trip?

◇ Pretty good. We chatted and enjoyed the landscape the whole way. You see, I like this country very much. / I'm afraid not. The air conditioning was so cold that I sneezed all the way.

◇ How do you do, Mr. Brown?

◇ Nice to meet you, Lynn.

◇ How was your trip?

◇ Did you enjoy your trip?

◇ How did your trip go? Did you enjoy it?

◇ Is this your first visit to China?

◇ Have you been to China before?

(4) Confirming numbers of the tourists/luggage.

◇ Could you tell me if everyone in the group is here, Mr. Williams?

Let me see. Yes, we are all here.

◇ Mr. Hugo, do we have all our guests here?

I'm sorry to say one couple didn't come due to sudden illness. We have 22 people now, including me.

◇ How many pieces of luggage do we have?

◇ May I have the baggage check, please?

Here you are. There are 12 pieces altogether.

◇ Can we get our luggage by the time we reach our hotel?

Absolutely. Actually, we'll go sightseeing right now. When we get to our hotel, I assure you that the luggage will be waiting for us there.

(5) Moving out of the airport/railway station.

◇ Could you tell the guests to follow my flag since it's so crowded here?

◇ Are we ready to go now?

◇ Yes, we are. Please hold your flag high so that we can see you.

◇ Our coach is waiting in the parking lot. The number is 88967, again, 88967. Please try to remember it, just in case you lose track of us.

(6) Offering help.

◇ Your bag seems quite heavy. May I help you with it?

No, thanks. I can manage it myself.

◇ It's a bit dark here. Take my hand and watch your step, please.

That's very kind of you, sweetie.

Module 5
On the Way to the Hotel

While reaching a new place, everything seems to be fresh, new and interesting to the tourists. They must be very curious about everything of the destination, so after meeting the tourists at the airport or railway station, the guide has the responsibility to introduce all kinds of things that the tourists might interested in. That means the tour guide should give a welcome speech, remind the tourists just from abroad to adjust the time, introduce the outside scene, as well as inform the bus number and the tour guide's mobile number.

Moreover, the guide should get ready to answer any questions that the visitors may ask. Concise and informative answers are most appreciated.

In addition, the guide should also check the number of the tour group before starting, and distribute pamphlets and copies of schedule after finishing his/her talk.

All of the above will surely help the guide to make an incredible first impression.

◇ Learning Objectives

Knowledge

① Know the service standard about the way to the hotel.

② Master the vocabulary and expressions about the way to the hotel.

Skills

① Be able to deliver a welcome speech warmly and properly.

② Be able to recognize and adjust the time difference.

③ Be able to conduct a tour on the way to the hotel.

④ Be able to give necessary reminders.

Quality

① Strengthen service consciousness and confidence.

② Foster self-study ability, problem-solving ability and presentation ability.

Task 1 Extending a welcome speech

◇Lead-in

Simon is assigned to serve the tour group CITS20161008A which will visit Changsha and Shaoshan from Oct. 8th to Oct. 10th. After a good preparation, Simon has received the tour group successfully at Huanghua International Airport around 4:30 p.m. Now, the bus is heading for Sheraton Changsha hotel. In order to make a good first impression, how should Simon deliver a welcome speech?

◇Analyzing the Task

Simon can successfully make a welcome speech as following.

① Prepare the welcome speech.

First, Simon should consider the nationality, age, education level, occupation, etc. of the tourists. Second, the welcome speech is usually delivered after the tourists just arrived, while during this period, the tourists are either too excited or too tired, the tour guide is not their focus. So, the welcome speech should be concise and to the point. Generally speaking, the time is better to be controlled in about 5 minutes.

In this task, the members of this tour group are students and teachers from the Confucius Institute in England. They know China a little, and are eager to know more about Hunan. Chinese proverbs showing hospitality can be included in the welcome speech.

② Be familiar with the welcome speech.

Practice well in advance, which will not only make Simon understand the content well, but also make him confident.

③ Extend the welcome speech.

First, dress neatly, and be energetic. Second, remember to smile, and be polite and calm. This can give the tourists a friendly and warm feeling. Third, be sure to speak naturally, clearly and confidently.

Module 5 On the Way to the Hotel

The on-the-spot communication is as following.

(G=the tour guide   L=the tour leader)

G: (On the bus, counting the tourists) Is everybody here? Our coach is about to start.

L: Yes, I think so.

G: Shall we go now?

L: Yes, please.

G: (to all the tourists in the coach) Good afternoon, ladies and gentlemen. Welcome to Hunan. Our bus is heading for the hotel now. It will take us about 30 minutes to get there. So, please just sit back and relax yourself. I am Simon, your local guide from Hunan China International Travel Service. And this is Mr. Li, our driver, who has 10 years of driving experience. On behalf of our company, we would like to extend our warm welcome to all of you. Welcome to Hunan. Confucius, the great ancient Chinese sage, once said "Isn't it a great pleasure to have friends coming from afar?" So it is my great happiness to be your guide in Hunan Province. During your stay here, I will be at your service at anytime and do everything possible to make your trip comfortable and enjoyable. Be sure to let me know if you have any problems, questions or suggestions, no matter what they are. And we highly appreciate your understanding and cooperation. Wish you a nice trip.

◇Developing Tasks

1. When traveling, how would you like the tour guide and the journey? Please use adjectives to describe.

_____

_____

_____

_____

2. Interpret the phrases.

致辞		舒适的	
	sit back	愉快的	
	relax yourself	合作	
随时为您服务		提前	
	be sure		appreciate

3. Please write down the language that can be used in the corresponding tasks.

Tasks	Language
On behalf of the travel agency, the guide welcome the tourists	
Tell the tourists the guides' name and the travel agency	
Introduce the driver	
Express sincere desire to serve the tourists	
Wish the tourists a good journey	

4. Listen and fill in the blanks.

Confucius, our ancient great ___①___ once said, "What a great joy it is to have friends from afar." Today, with such great ___②___, on ___③___ of China International Travel Service, Beijing, one of the largest and best travel ___④___ in China, I'd like to extend our ___⑤___ welcome to all of you, our ___⑥___ guests from the other side of the Pacific.

I also hope that during your short stay in Beijing, you not only can ___⑦___ your eyes and stomach, but also ___⑧___ the real Chinese culture and have a better ___⑨___ of the Chinese people and its ongoing reforms, which ___⑩___ the greatness of China.

5. Simulation

Mary is the local guide of the Zhangjiajie Branch of CITS. She is receiving a foreign tour group of 43 from Japan at 7:00 from the airport. The group will stay in Zhangjiajie from March 8th to 10th. Suppose you are Mary, try to make a welcome speech to them on the way to the hotel.

Task 2　Adjusting to the time difference

◇Lead-in

Simon is receiving the tour group CITS20161008A at 16:00 from the airport. Being their first stop, how should Simon help the tourists adjust to the time difference?

Analyzing the Task

Help the guests adjust the time difference.

The on-the-spot communication is as following.

(G=the tour guide　　T=the tourists)

G: As you see, Beijing Time is the standard time in China. It's 8 hours ahead of London Time. For example, when it is 12 at noon in Beijing, the standard time in London is 4 a.m. And now it is 4:00 p.m. Oct. 8th, Beijing Time, please adjust your watch to 4:00 p.m. Is it OK now?

T: Yes.

G: Thank you. I know some of you may suffer from the jet lag, which may cause you feel tired or even ill, so we have no activities this evening. You can have a good rest in the hotel. And I really hope you can adjust the jet lag as soon as possible.

Developing Tasks

1. When it is 8 a.m. in China, what's the time in the following cities? Please write down.

City	Time
Tokyo	
Seoul	
Bangkok	
Singapore	
London	

City	Time
Berlin	
Paris	
New York	
Sydney	
Male	

2. Interpret the phrases.

北京标准时间		时区	
时差		适应时差	
遭受			jet lag
	local time		Eastern Hemisphere
晚于		早于	
	behind		ahead of

3. Try to translate the following sentences.

① 东京和伦敦的时差是多少?

② 北京比伦敦早 8 个小时。

③ 我们这里是北京时间。

④ Jet lag never really bothers me.

⑤ I always have trouble with jet lag.

4. Listen and fill in the blanks.

We will always __①__ you in __②__ when we will meet to go somewhere and when we will have our meals. It's very important that you always try to be __③__. To __④__ that we don't have any problems, I'd like to remind you of the __⑤__. While you are __⑥__ in China, you will always use Beijing __⑦__ Time. Right now it is September 20th and the __⑧__ time is 10:00 a.m. Please __⑨__ your watches now, so that we can avoid any __⑩__ later on.

5. Simulation.

Mr. Brown and his family are the guests from Korea. Lily is the local guide from Hunan Overseas International Travel Service (HOTC). On the way to the hotel, how should Lily help them adjust to the time difference?

Task 3　Guiding on the Way

◇Lead-in

Simon, the local guide, welcomes the tour group CITS20161008A from the airport warmly. The guests are students and teachers from the Confucius Institute in England, and have known some information about China, but this is their first time to Changsha and Hunan. On the way to Sheraton Changsha, the guests want to know much about Hunan and Changsha, so how does Simon make a great guiding?

◇ Analyzing the Task

Simon must do the following.

① Be familiar with the route.

The route starts from Changsha Huanghua International Airport, along Changyong expressway, the Window of the World, Hunan International Convention & Exhibition Center, the West Lake Building Restaurant, Sifangping Overpass, Wujialing and Sheraton Changsha at the end. It will take 40 minutes to get to the hotel.

② Prepare the tour commentaries.

First, the introduction should be given throughout the whole way as the whole journey is about 40 minutes. Second, the introduction should cover the scenery along the way and the general situation of Hunan. Third, the content should be concise and interesting since the coach is fast and the tourists are curious.

③ Conduct the tour guiding.

a. Stand in the front of the coach, the right back of the driver.

b. The facial expressions must be natural, with a smile.

c. Use moderate volume and pace; be sure every tourist hears clearly.

The on-the-spot communication is as following.

(G=the tour guide   L=the tour leader   T=the tourists)

G: Is everybody here, Mr. Brown? The driver is ready to start the coach.

L: Yes, everyone is on the coach. We can go now.

G: (on the way to the hotel) Ladies and gentlemen, welcome to Hunan. Please allow me to introduce myself. My name is Simon. I'm a guide from Hunan China International Travel Service. I'm glad to have all of you here. I'll be with you in the following 3 days of the tour. And this is Mr. Liu, our driver. He is responsible and experienced. We'll do everything possible to make your visit a pleasant experience. If you have any problems or suggestions, please don't hesitate to let us know. Now we're on our way to the hotel where you are going to stay, Sheraton Changsha.

T: How far is it?

G: It will take us about 30 minutes to get there. You may as well have a glimpse at the outskirt and the city along the way.

T: How is the hotel?

G: It's one of the best international five-star hotels in the city, with a full range of outstanding facilities. And the service is warm and efficient there. The hotel is situated in the center of the city. It has easy access to many places of interests, shopping malls and entertainment centers in Changsha. I hope you'll enjoy your stay there.

T: That's great!

G: The airport you just arrived at is Changsha Huanghua International Airport, which is the largest and most modern civil airport in Hunan Province. It was built in 1989, and now the annual passenger capacity is nearly 10 million. The road we are on now is Changyong expressway. It is completed in 1996, 22.25 kilometers long. And the maximum speed limit is 120 km an hour.

T: This is our first trip to Changsha. We have been looking forward to seeing the city.

G: Since you'll have a whole day to visit Changsha tomorrow, and Changsha is the provincial capital of Hunan, so here I'd like to introduce the scenery along the way and the general situation of Hunan.

Hunan, meaning a place south to the Dongting Lake, is short for Xiang, because of its longest river, River Xiang, and is also called "the Kingdom of Hibiscus" due to the widely planted hibiscus. Hunan covers an area of 211,800 square kilometers, governs 14 prefectures, borders 6 administrative regions: to the east is Jiangxi Province, the south are Guangdong Province and Guangxi Zhuang Autonomous Region, the west are Guizhou and Chongqing, the north is Hubei Province. So Hunan is an important province in the middle of China.

Hunan boasts rich tourism resources with numerous historic relics, colourful folklore and beautiful scenery, such as Hunan's historical and cultural city Changsha, the world famous and fascinating attraction—Mawangdui Han Tombs, one of the China's Five Sacred Mountains—Mt. Hengshan, the former residence of Chairman Mao, the world-class natural heritage—the natural landscapes of Wulingyuan and Langshan Mountain, China's second largest freshwater lake—the Dongting Lake, the one-thousand-year institution of higher learning—Yuelu Academy, the long and narrow island—Orange Island Park, the famous historic and cultural city—Phoenix Ancient Town, which was ever praised as "the most beautiful small city in China" by Rewi Alley, a renowned author in New Zealand.

T: My god. What an amazing place!

G: Hunan cuisine is also worth a taste. Hunan cuisine, one of the eight major styles of cooking in China, is characterized by its strong and spicy flavor, which is totally different form the flavor in your country. There is a common saying "Sichuan people don't fear hot food, Hunan people don't fear any degree of spiciness at all, and Guizhou people fear to eat food that isn't spicy." The famous dishes are Crispy Duck, Dong'an Chicken, Steamed Fish Head with Chopped Peppers, Lotus Seeds in Sugar Candy. The featured snacks are Stinky Tofu, Sister Rice Balls in Fire Palace.

T: That sounds tasty. We'd like to have a try.

G: I'm sure the delicious local food won't disappoint any guests. Now we are in the center of Changsha County, also named Xingsha, one of the suburban counties of Changsha City. Changsha County is among the Top Hundred Counties in China, and has two national level development zones.

After getting off the expressway, we enter the downtown area of Changsha City, which is divided into 5 districts. They are Kaifu District in the north where we are staying now, Yuelu District in the west, Yuhua District in the south, Furong District in the east, and Tianxin District in the center.

T: Which district is the hotel in?

G: Kaifu District. Ladies and gentlemen, please look to your right. This is the Window of the World in Changsha, which is a theme park with micro-landscape. The large building near it is Hunan International Convention & Exhibition Center. The opening ceremony of the famous China Golden Eagle TV Art Festival is held in this building every year. This festival is the only national comprehensive award for TV art voted by the masses, which attracts a wide range of participants as well as the attention of overseas media with its worldwide reputation. Many A-listers will attend the festival.

T1: Wow! Being such a magnificent event, it must attract a lot people.

T2: What about that group of palace buildings? Did the emperor once lived there?

G: NO, it isn't. It is the largest restaurant in Asia, the West Lake Building, which is listed in the Guinness World Records. The restaurant is famous for Hunan cuisine, and has a capacity of 4,000 people eating there. The layout is a pattern of the Forbidden City in Beijing, and the scenery copies Suzhou Gardens. And it is an outdoor shooting base, too.

T: It's gorgeous and elaborate, indeed.

G: In the opposite of the West Lake Building, there is a building shaped like H. It is the headquarter of Hunan Broadcasting Group. The television industry of Changsha is really developed. Hunan TV is known as "Hunan Television Army", and ranked as the top three satellite TV in China because of its high audience rating. A series of famous shows developed by Hunan TV, such as Happy Camp, Super Girl, Happy boy, Where Are We Going, Dad? I Am a Singer, greatly increase the influence at home and abroad.

T: I have watched I Am a Singer. It's really great. I love it.

G: We are now on Furong Road. Furong Road is a main road running through south and north. It is a finance street where there are many financial institutions. Furong Road has become the longest urban road in 2003 in China. Our hotel is on Furong Road, too. Can you see the tall building on the right side? That's Sheraton Changsha.

T: Here we are.

G: Now we've arrived at our hotel. Please gather your belongings and follow me.

◇ Developing Tasks

1. Please match the tourist attractions with the corresponding pictures.

a. Yuelu Academy   b. Zhangjiajie National Forest Park

c. Hunan Museum   d. Heng Mountain

e. Orange Island   f. Former Residence of Mao Zedong

g. Phoenix Ancient Town   h. Yueyang Tower & Dongting Lake

i. Window of the World

2. Interpret the phrases.

音量适中		第二大	
五星级酒店			border
	glimpse	旅游胜地	
	outskirt	当提到……	
高速公路			cuisine
期望		县	
	development zone	世界自然遗产	
荣誉,名声			A-lister

3. Listen and fill in the blanks.

A tour guide should first have the ___①___ language that his customers use. When you have the sufficient language ___②___, your customers will feel that they can share the atmosphere easily.

Language plays an important part in a culture. One's cultural background determines his ___③___ style. Our native language is Chinese, so our thinking style is different from the ___④___ people. You need to practice the corresponding language until you can use it to the satisfaction of your tourists.

Being a tour guide, one will have a lot of chances to talk in public. So you need public speaking skill. If you are so ___⑤___ when you stand up, it is not very good because nobody wants to see a frightened face with ___⑥___ manners. You are required to ___⑦___ at the listeners evenly; your ___⑧___ should be clear and loud enough for everybody to hear. Your ___⑨___ of speaking is as important as your volume, because if you talk too fast, people cannot follow. Additionally, your facial expression, gesture, posture and ___⑩___ will all help the listener to understand you.

4. Complete the dialogue.

(G＝the guide;B ＝ Mr. Black)

G: ①_____,(所有人都在这吗？) Mr. Black? The driver is ready to start the coach.

B: Yes, everyone is on the coach. We can go now.

G:(On the way to the hotel)Ladies and gentlemen, welcome to Beijing. First, let me introduce myself. My name is Cheng Guo. Cheng is my family name. ②_____
_____.(你们参观北京期间,我将担任你们的地陪导游) This is Mr. Zhou, our

driver. ③_____(周先生是一个有责任心又有经验的司机), so you are in good hands when riding in his coach. To avoid getting on a wrong bus, we'd better remember the number and the features of our bus. The number is 2066890. If you have any special interest, please let me know. My job is to smooth your way, care for your welfare, and try my best to answer your questions. ④_____. (真心感谢各位的理解与合作)

B: How far is it to the hotel?

G: About a fifty-minute ride. ⑤_____. (您不妨顺便沿途观赏一下这个城市的景色)

B: Yes, I have been looking forward to seeing the city. I know there are many spots and historical sites in Beijing, such as the Great Wall, the Imperial Palace, and the Summer Palace. I am really itching for a visit.

G: ⑥_____. (经过长途旅行,你一定很累了) I think you should have a good rest before we get down to sightseeing.

B: OK, I am here at your disposal. Oh, that must be Tian'anmen. I know it can date back to the Ming dynasty. The square is so wonderful!

G: It is 440,000 square meters, ⑦_____. (是当今世界上最大的广场之一) The seven bridges in front of Tian'anmen are called Golden Water Bridges. In ancient times, only the emperor and empress could walk on the bridge in the center.

B: That's rather interesting. What about that building?

G: ⑧_____. (那座宏伟的建筑包括两个博物馆) The northern half is the Museum of Chinese Revolution, and the southern half is the Museum of Chinese History. In the center of the square is the Monument to the People's Heroes.

B: What do the Chinese characters in its north face mean?

G: "Eternal Glory to the People's Heroes!" They are Chairman Mao's calligraphy. ⑨_____. (碑的南面是毛主席纪念堂)

B: I see. I think the splendid building on the west side must be the Great Hall of the People.

G: Yes. The Chinese leaders often meet foreign guests there. Many important issues are discussed in that building. And many national policies and legislations are also made there.

B: Now I know why this place is called the heart of China. By the way, can I know the schedule you have planned for us?

G: We are ready to hear your suggestions. I'm sure we'll have enough time to see the city. I'll be very glad to show you around.

B: Thank you.

G: Well, here we are. This is the hotel. ⑩_____. (让我们下车到总台登记吧)

5. Simulation.

A tour group of 30 from Australia will travel in Hunan from July 15th to July 20th. The arrival time is 18:00. Nancy is the local guide from CITS. She is taking the tour group from Changsha railway station to Preess Resort & Hotel. Suppose you are Nancy, please make a tour guiding on the way to the hotel.

Task 4　Warm reminding

◇Lead-in

Simon, the local guide, is taking the tour group from the airport to the hotel. This is their first meeting. What and how does Simon remind the guests?

◇Analyzing the Task

Simon can remind the guests as follows.

"During your stay in Hunan, I'd like to remind you of some important things. First, we are a group of 20 people. Please be punctual during the travel. Otherwise we will waste time. Second, please stay healthy. Don't drink tap water in the hotel. We should drink mineral water. And the temperature changes dramatically in fall. So it is necessary to take a coat with you when going out. Third, I hope you will remember the bus number Xiang A-862525 since we will spend a lot of time with the bus. Let me repeat it, Xiang A-862525. And my mobile number is 18153794789, 18153794789. I would have it on 24 hours. Please don't hesitate to call me whenever necessary. The last thing is to take good care of your personal belongings, including your handbag, passport, wallet and camera."

◇Developing Tasks

1. What should you remind your guests as a tour guide at your first meeting? Please choose the items from the following list.

☐ be punctual ☐ stay healthy ☐ bus number ☐ personal belongings

☐ meeting time ☐ meeting place ☐ weather ☐ guide's mobile number

☐ travel agency ☐ driver's name ☐ time difference ☐ drink mineral water

☐ dress ☐ schedule ☐ use electricity transformer

2. Interpret the phrases.

提醒		车牌号码	
遵守时间安排			hesitate
	stay healthy		take a good care of
20人的团队		个人物品	
自来水		手机号码	

3. Try to translate the following sentences.

① 在湖南停留期间,我有 4 件重要的事要提醒你们。

② 春天天气多变,外出时请携带外套。

③ 请随时保管好随身携带的行李物品。

④ In order to avoid unnecessary problems, please be punctual during your travel.

⑤ I would have it on 24 hours. Please don't hesitate to call me whenever you are in need.

4. Simulation.

A tour group of 28 from Russia will travel in Hunan from July 20th to July 24th. Lily is the local guide, and she meets the guests at 7:00pm from Huanghua International Airport. Now she is taking the group from the airport to Preess Resort & Hotel. Suppose you are Lily, please give a warm reminding.

◇ Related Knowledge

1. Things should be done on the way from the airport to the hotel.

① Check the number of the tour group.

② Head for the hotel with the permission of the tour leader and the national guide.

③ Extend a warm welcome speech.

④ Inform the overseas tourists of the local time.

⑤ Guide on the way: introduce the scene on the way, local condition and situation in the hotel.

⑥ Provide some necessary reminding.

2. Main points in a welcome speech.

① Be on behalf of the travel agency, the driver and yourself to welcome the tourists.

② Tell the tourists your name and your travel agency.

③ Introduce the driver.

④ Express your sincere desire to serve the tourists.

⑤ Wish the tourists a good journey.

3. A welcome speech example.

Good evening, ladies and gentlemen.

Welcome to China! Welcome to Shanghai.

Confucius, our great ancient philosopher once said, "What a great joy it is to have friends from afar!" Today, with such great joy, on behalf of China Youth Travel Service, I'd like to express a warm welcome to all of you, our distinguished guests from the other side of the Pacific. I also hope that during your short stay in Shanghai, you not only satisfy your eyes and stomach, but also experience the real Chinese culture and have a better understanding of the Chinese people.

Please allow me to say a few words about myself. My name is Gao Yuan. You can simply call me Gao, which means "tall" in Chinese, although I'm not tall at all. This is our driver, Mr. Li, who has been driving for more than ten years. Mr. Li and I will be at your disposal. We will do everything possible to make your visit a pleasant experience. If you have any problems or requests, please do not hesitate to let us know.

You are going to stay at Shangri-La Hotel, a luxurious, five-star hotel located right on the famous Huangpu River. Since you are to stay in our city for two days, you will be using this vehicle during your stay in Shanghai. So please take trouble to jot down the plate number for future convenience: 8E199. I will repeat: 8E199. Got it?

Known throughout the world as the "Pearl of the Orient", Shanghai is a modern and fast-paced city, rich in history and culture, which has a wealth of areas and sites just waiting to be explored. During the following two days, you will experience the old part of the city by investigating Shanghai's former concession(租界)areas and Yuyuan Garden. You will also visit the newest area of the city, Pudong, and two of its most impressive structures: Jinmao Tower and the Oriental Pearl TV Tower. In addition, tomorrow evening you will take a cruise on the Huangpu River and enjoy the beautiful night scenery on both sides.

I sincerely wish you a pleasant, comfortable stay and a fantastic holiday here. I shall do all I can to make everything easy for you.

Thank you and have an enjoyable evening!

4. Help FIT adjust time difference.

(G=the tour guide   S=Mr. Smith   L=Lucy)

Mr. Smith and his wife Lucy are guests from London. This is their first trip to China. Wang Li, a guide from Beijing International Travel Service welcomes them warmly. On the way to the hotel, Wan Li helps them adjust to the time difference.

L: What is the time you use here?

G: We are on Beijing Time. Beijing Time is the standard time for the whole country.

S: What time is it now in Beijing?

G: It is 11:30 a.m. Beijing Time now.

S: I have to adjust my watch to the local time. We have just come from London and we are not used to the time difference here at all.

L: What's the time difference between Beijing and London?

G: Chinese time is 8 hours ahead of London in England. When it is 12 at noon in Beijing, the standard time in London is 4 a.m.

S: OK, I see. Thank you for the information. Without your help, I would have no idea about what time it is.

G: My pleasure. Well, we now arrive at Beijing Hotel. A number of antique stores are behind the hotel. And in the evening, there are dozens of stalls there and it turns the street into an antique market.

W: That is terrific.

L: I hope you will enjoy your stay here.

5. Main points of guiding on the way.

On the way to the hotel, the tour guide should give the tourists information including:

① The scenery along the way to the hotel. When introducing the scenery along the way, tour guides must react quickly and be well-timed. The content must be concise, attractive, and the explaining rhythm must match the speed of the coach.

② The local customs. The local customs should be interspersed into the scenery introduction. Remember, never detail the scenic spots included in the itinerary.

③ The destination they are going to arrive at. A brief introduction of the arriving destination should be given, too.

④ The hotel they are going to stay in. The information like the hotel name, grade, size, facilities, location, transportation can be referred.

6. Time of guiding on the way.

The time of the introduction on the way to the hotel depends on the distance, and the details are showed below:

Distance of driving	Time of introducing
less than 30 minutes	throughout the whole way
more than 30 minutes but less than 2 hours	occupy 50%-60% of the whole way
more than 2 hours	decided by the local guide, but at least occupy 10% of the whole way

7. A glimpse of Hunan Province.

Hunan, literally means south of the lake. Hunan Province is called Hunan because it is located south of the Dongting Lake, in the middle of the Yangtze River. It is said that there was a large area of hibiscus in Hunan in the past, so that Hunan is also called the hometown of hibiscus. It is also called "Xiang" for short as the Xiangjiang River zigzags through it. Hunan covers a total area of over 210,000 square kilometers, and has a population of nearly 70 million. It is surrounded by mountains on the east, the south and the west. The Dongting Lake and other plain lakes are scattered in the north. It is known as the Land of Plenty. The transportation is convenient as there are six major national railway lines and 5 airports in Hunan.

Climate of Hunan

Hunan is located in the region of continental subtropical seasonal humid climate. It has four distinct seasons, long frostless periods and abundant rain.

The best time to travel in Hunan is in spring and autumn, especially from April to June. Spring in Hunan is short and rainy, and the weather changes a lot in this season.

Summer is long and extremely hot in Hunan. The average temperature is higher than 28 ℃. Hunan is very dry and cool in autumn. The average temperature seems to be 16 ℃-19 ℃. In winter, it is a little cold in Hunan. The average temperature of the coldest month January may be 4 ℃-7 ℃.

Nations of Hunan

Hunan is a multi-ethnic province. The major ethnic groups are Han Chinese as well as the Tujia, Miao, Dong, Yao, Hui, Uygur and Zhuang ethnic minorities.

Historical figures of Hunan

A large number of outstanding figures come from Human Province, so the province enjoys the reputation of "the Kingdom of Chu, the unique home of talented people". For example, Cai Lun invented papermaking technology which has been honored as one of ancient China's "Four Great Inventions". Zhou Dunyi is the founder of the Confucian school of idealist philosophy in the Song and Ming dynasties. Wang Fuzhi is an outstanding 17th century Chinese philosopher.

The outstanding figures in the Chinese modern history include Wei Yuan, Zeng Guofan, He Shaoji, Zuo Zongtang, Tan Sitong, Chen Tianhua, Huang Xing and Song Jiaoren.

From the May Fourth Movement to the New Democratic Revolution or even to the socialist revolution and construction period, a great number of Party leaders, government officials and military figures emerged from this province. The most outstanding representatives are Mao Zedong, Cai Hesen, Ren Bishi, Liu Shaoqi, Peng Dehuai, He Long, and Luo Ronghuan. Meanwhile, a large group of talented writers, artists, scientists and educators have hailed from Hunan Province. These figures include Qi Baishi (the great master of Chinese painting), Tian Han (the famous playwright), and the well-known writers Shen Congwen and Zhou Libo.

Recommended attractions in Hunan

Hunan is a major tourist region, with rich tourism resources. The attractions worth visiting are Yuelu Mountain Scenic Resorts and Historical Sites, Hunan Provincial Museum, Emperor Yan's Mausoleum, Chairman Mao zedong's former residence, Nanyue Heng Mountain, Langshan Scenic Area, Yueyang Tower, Peach Blossom Garden, Suxian Mountain, Fenghuang Ancient Town, Wulingyuan Scenic Area, Yuelu Academy.

Hunan cuisine

Hunan cuisine, sometimes called Xiang cuisine, is one of the eight regional cuisines of China and is well known for its hot spicy flavor, fresh aroma and deep colors. Hunan food is hot because the climate in Hunan is very humid, which makes it difficult for the human body to eliminate moisture. The local people eat hot peppers to help remove dampness.

The representative dishes are Dong'an Chicken, Mao's Braised Port with Soy Sauce, Quick-Fried Julienne Ox Tripe, Lotus Seeds in Rock Sugar Syrup, Stir-fried Chicken with Hot Chillies, Steamed Fish Head in Chopped Pepper, Steamed Multiple Preserved Ham, Yongzhou Blood Duck and so on.

Chairman Mao once claimed that "the more chillies one eats, the more revolutionary one becomes". It is a joke but the statement illustrates the Chinese belief that diet makes a great difference to a person's personality.

8. A brief introduction of Changsha.

Changsha, the capital of Hunan Province, is a famous ancient city with a history of 3,500 years. It used to be a place of strategic importance in the Kingdom of Chu, and a famous prefecture of the Qin dynasty (221 BC-207 BC). Now Changsha is an important city with historical and cultural relics, and an ideal destination of tourism or sightseeing at home and abroad.

Changsha sits at the northeast of Hunan Province, boasts a total area of 11,819 km^2, governs six districts, two counties and one city, and owns five national development zones.

The name of Changsha was first seen in the West Zhou dynasty 3,000 years ago. In later dynasties, Changsha was always an important city of Hunan and a key town in Southern China. In 1982, Changsha was reckoned among the first group of 24 historical cities in China by the State Council of China. As a result of more than 20 years' reform and opening, tremendous changes have taken place in Changsha.

Tour in Changsha

Changsha boasts a large number of historical and cultural relics, of which the West Han Tombs excavated in Mawangdui and the Inscribed Bamboo Slips of Sun Wu from the Three Kingdoms Period uncovered in Zoumalou have shocked the world. Tianxin Pavilion, the symbol of ancient Changsha, witnessed the historical development and changes of Changsha. Yuelu Acamedy, one of the four most famous academies in China, is widely accepted to be among the oldest academies in the world.

Changsha is closely related to a great number of great figures in both ancient and modern history of China, including Qu Yuan, Jia Yi, Zhu Xi, Zeng Guofan, Mao Zedong, Huangxing, Cai E, Liu shaoqi, Hu Yaobang, and former prime minister Zhu

Rongji.

Changsha is also a beautiful city. There are many natural scenic spots, including Mount Yuelu which is pregnant with beauty and vitality, the Xiangjiang River that flows through the whole city from south to north with the picturesque Orange Isle quietly lying in it. All these jointly compose a melodious song.

Snacks in Changsha

Coming to Changsha, what you can't miss most is the delicious snacks which own unique charm. The most representative snacks are Stinky Tofu, Rice Cake Fried in Syrup as well as Tasty Shrimp. In addition, rice noodles of Changsha in breakfast time is the most popular food.

9. Four important things to remind guests.

① Be punctual.

② Stay healthy.

③ Remember the bus number and the guide's mobile number.

④ Take good care of their personal belongings.

10. Useful sentences.

(1) A welcome speech.

◇ Ladies and gentlemen, may I have your attention, please? Thank you.

◇ Please just sit back and relax yourself.

◇ Let me introduce... to...

◇ Please allow me to introduce... to you.

◇ My name is... My English name is... You can just call me...

◇ On behalf of CYTS, I'd like to extend our warm welcome to all of you.

◇ Isn't it a great pleasure to have friends coming from afar?

◇ During your stay here, I will be at your service at anytime and do everything possible to make your trip comfortable and enjoyable.

◇ I will try my best to make your journey interesting and unforgettable.

◇ Be sure to let me know if you have any problems, questions or suggestions, no matter what they are.

◇ We highly appreciate your understanding and cooperation.

◇ I sincerely wish you a pleasant and comfortable stay and a fantastic holiday here.

(2) Adjust to time difference.

◇ Beijing time is the standard time for the whole country.

◇ While you are traveling in China, you will always use Beijing time.

◇ Beijing time is 13 hours ahead of New York time.

◇ Please adjust your watch to 4:00 p. m.

◇ What's the local time now?

◇ Right now it is September 20th and the current time is 10:00 a. m. Please adjust your watches now.

◇ Please set your watch by the local time.

◇ Are you still suffering from jet lag?

(3) Guiding on the way.

◇ About a fifty-minute ride.

◇ It will take us about 30 minutes to get there.

◇ You may as well have a glimpse at the outskirts and the city along the way.

◇ Ladies and gentlemen, let's now take a brief look at the sights outside.

◇ It has easy access to many places of interests, shopping malls and entertainment centers.

◇ The recorded history of Changsha can be traced back to 3,000 years ago.

◇ Hunan is located in the south of the Dongting Lake, and the name derives from the location.

◇ Wuyi Avenue was founded in 1951, and so it got its name.

◇ Hunan is sometimes called Xiang for short, after the Xiang River which runs through the province.

◇ Hunan covers an area of 211,800 square kilometers, and borders 6 administrative regions.

◇ Hunan has a population of 69 million.

◇ Hunan Province is famous for its picturesque scenery.

◇ Hunan cuisine is characterized by its strong and spicy flavor.

◇ After getting off the expressway, we enter the downtown area of Changsha.

◇ Ladies and gentlemen, please look on your right.

◇ This festival attracts a wide range of participants as well as the attention of overseas media.

◇ Can you see the tall building on the right side? That's Sheraton Changsha Hotel.

◇ Please gather your belongings and follow me.

◇ Let's get off and go to the reception desk.

(4) Warm reminding.

◇ Now I'd like to remind you of some important things.

◇ In order to avoid unnecessary problems, please be punctual during your travel.

◇ The weather in spring is changeable, so it is necessary to take a coat with you when going out.

◇ Since you travel in the hot summer season, I suggest you wear your hats and sunglasses on tour.

◇ As you are tourists and you are not familiar with the surrounding of Chengdu, you need to remember the number of the coach, as well as my phone number.

◇ I would have it on 24 hours. Please don't hesitate to call me whenever you are in need.

◇ Please write down the license plate number of the coach.

Module 6
At the Hotel

The hotel is a temporary home for people who are travelling. Therefore, hotels play an important role on the journey. Consequently, prior to greeting the guests, the guide should contact with the hotel and confirm the guests' reservation, including the number of rooms, the types of rooms and so on, to make sure that the guests will check in smoothly. And during their stay at the hotel, the guide should liaise with the hotel to provide all kinds of services and take good care of the guests until their itinerary ends up.

◇Learning Objectives

Knowledge

① Learn about the procedures of checking in at the hotel.

② Be familiar with the hotel facilities and service.

③ Master the vocabulary, useful expressions and sentences used in check-in.

Skills

① Be able to help the guests to check in and deal with the formalities.

② Be able to introduce the hotel service and facilities to the guests.

③ Be able to make a wake-up call.

Quality

① Strengthen logic thinking ability and language expressive ability.

② Be familiar with the tourism industry, and improve service consciousness and confidence.

Task 1　Checking in

◇Lead-in

After a long flight journey, the tourists feel very tired, therefore, after arriving at the hotel, the tour guide should assist the hotel receptionist to arrange the tourists quickly. In order to make the tourists live comfortable enough to go on with the trip, how should Simon do to help the 20 tourists settle down fast and well?

◇Analyzing the Task

The procedure of checking in for group guests should be as follows.

① As usual, there will be a tour leader in the group, and he will have a group visa, and the necessary information of the guests are shown on it, so it's unnecessary for the guests to show their passports at the hotel.

② The tour guide should communicate with the clerk at the front desk first and make sure he can get the right rooms.

③ Help the guests with the formalities. Simon must be familiar with the registration form, because sometimes the hotel clerk will ask the guests to fill in the form by themselves.

④ Ask the tour leader to show his group visa to the front desk, and the clerk at the front desk will make a copy of it.

⑤ Help the tour leader distribute the rooms. Before showing the room keys to the guests, the guide should remind them of the necessary information of the rest arrangement.

The on-the-spot communication is as following.

(R＝the receptionist　　S＝Simon　　T＝the tourist)

R: Good morning! Welcome to our hotel! Can I help you?

S: Good morning! We are a tour group of 22 people. I'm the tour guide of the group. My name is Simon, from China International Travel Service. We reserved 10 rooms the day before yesterday.

R: Just a minute, please. I'll check the reservation record.

(She speaks again after checking the reservation record.)

R: Yes, we have a record of your reservation here. It is 8 twin-bed rooms, 2 single rooms, starting today. And you're scheduled to check out on October 10th. Is that right?

S: Yes, you're right.

R: Your rooms are 901 and 908 for twin-bed rooms, 909 and 910 for single rooms. Would you like to fill in the registration forms for the group, please?

S: Sure. Thank you. By the way, the rate of the rooms is 580 yuan per room per night. Is that right?

R: Yes, that's right.

S: Here are the completed registration forms.

R: Thanks. May I see your ID cards, please?

G: Certainly.

(Simon and the tourists show their ID cards to the receptionist.)

R: Thanks. And here are the keys for the rooms.

S: Thank you. Is there a telephone in each room?

R: Yes, all of our rooms have phones. You can make IDD calls and send faxes or telegrams in the hotel. If you need any assistance, please call the front desk.

T: That's wonderful. We would like to call our families tonight.

S: The hotel also offers money exchange service and laundry service.

T: I think we'd all like to have a bath and change our clothes.

R: If you want to have your clothes washed, just put them in the laundry bag in your bath room. It will be collected in the morning and returned the following morning. If you are ready now, the bellboy will take you to your rooms.

S: OK. Let's go to see our rooms.

Developing Tasks

1. In what order will the following procedures be served in checking in?

   a. Make sure about the room type the tourists need and help the tourists with the formalities (such as the registration form).

   b. Tell some specific information (such as the number of the guests, the number of the rooms, the name of the travel agency, the name of the person who reserves the rooms...etc.) of the tourists to the front desk.

c. Help the tourists solve some other problems immediately and actively.

d. Remind the tourists to get their passports ready (the group guests will have a group visa).

e. Tell them the location of the elevator, the time and the place for assembling and other necessary information.

f. Explain all kinds of information to help the tourists to check in.

g. Put the room numbers on the luggage and have the luggage sent to the rooms as soon as possible, after the luggage arrives at the hotel.

2. Listening practice.

Listen to the following dialogue and try to answer the following questions.

Hotel Check-in

① What is the first problem with the man's reservation?

A. The hotel confused him with another guest.

B. Rooms are overbooked for that evening.

C. There are no more rooms available for five people.

D. The price for the room is more than he expected.

② For what day did Mr. Nelson make a hotel reservation?

A. The eighteenth.

B. The nineteenth.

C. The twentieth.

D. The twenty-first.

③ What is taking place in the city that makes getting another room almost impossible?

A. A marathon.

B. An outdoor music festival.

C. A conference.

D. Building renovation.

④ How much is the initial discount on the honeymoon suite after Mr. Nelson complains about the hotel service?

A. $10.

B. $15.

C. $20.

D. $25.

⑤ How does Mr. Nelson respond when the hotel clerk offers to provide him with a free room on his next visit?

A. He thinks it will take a long time for him to receive the free coupon for the room.

B. He feels he should first receive an apology from the manager for what has happened.

C. He suggests that the hotel should give guests an additional 15% discount in cases like his.

D. He implies that he might not visit again because of the problems he has had.

3. Fill in the blanks.

Fill in the blanks with the given words below. Change the form where necessary.

check	registration	schedule	sign	confirm
deliver	settle	reserve	possible	account

① We arrived at the airport, our baggage _____ and wandered around the gift shops.

② After a long wait, some of them finally get to stay and _____ down, while others have to pack up and leave for a new destination.

③ I was writing my _____ at the bottom of the page.

④ I walk around with my head up because I know deep down inside that nothing is _____ if you try.

⑤ I told him my main _____ about his film was the ending.

⑥ Travel arrangements are subject to _____ by the head office.

⑦ No one will believe those promises because they know that later it will not be in _____ your interest to.

⑧ The _____ of the university shows an increase of 10 percent over last year.

⑨ We must always go into the whys and wherefores of anything. On no _____ should we follow anyone like sheep.

⑩ A tight _____ means we can't delay any longer.

4. Match.

Match the words to their collocations, then complete the sentences with them.

advance	out
ask	or
check	in
either	with
fill	for

① However, once you have agreed to the initial request, they would begin to _____ more.

② I turn from my work and my eyes _____ the mist.

③ Dress appropriately for your date, and you should probably let your date know _____ where you are planning to take her so she can also dress appropriately.

④ If not _____, you have to report yourself to make sure.

⑤ So whereas deduction is an _____ thing and induction is a matter of degree.

Task 2　Introducing Hotel Facilities

◇Lead-in

Some of the tourists want to hang out around the hotel after dinner, and ask Simon about the hotel. How should Simon introduce to the tourists about the hotel facilities and the nearby surroundings?

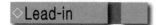

① Greet the guests in a warm and polite manner.

② Introduce the main service items and facilities to the guests.

③ Introduce the charge of the items and the way of payment.

④ Remind the guests about security problems.

The on-the-spot communication is as following.

(A＝the guest　　B＝Simon)

A: Excuse me. Could you tell us some details about the hotel we're staying?

B: Sure. What would you like to know?

A: Does the hotel have a swimming pool? My daughter loves swimming.

B: Yes, the hotel not only has a very lovely swimming pool with sun decks, but also has a children's pool which is specially designed for kids.

A: That's great. Does the hotel have a fitness facility?

B: Yes, Madam. It's gratis. Just take your room key and you can get in.

A: Good. How about Wi-Fi? Do I get Wi-Fi in my room?

B: Yes, the hotel provides free Wi-Fi service in public areas and our bedrooms.

A: That will be great. By the way, does the hotel have a shuttle bus to the airport?

B: I'm very sorry that the hotel does not have a shuttle bus. You can take the metro to the airport, and we are just 5-minute walk from the metro. You can't miss it.

A: Where can I do some shopping for souvenirs?

B: You might try the Patong Beach Street.

A: OK, thank you for your information.

B: My pleasure.

◇ Developing Tasks

1. Match the hotel terms with the correct Chinese.

The following is a list of words related to hotel terms. After reading it, you are required to find the Chinese equivalents in the table below. You should put corresponding letters in the brackets.

A. mini bar　　　　　　　　　　B. multi-function room

C. 24-hour room service　　　　　D. 24-hour business centre

E. youth hostel　　　　　　　　　F. wake-up service

G. shuttle van to / from the airport　H. souvenir shop

I. tour coordinator　　　　　　　　J. terminal hotel

K. tea trolley　　　　　　　　　　L. seasonality

M. safe　　　　　　　　　　　　N. room with good ventilation

O. recreation department　　　　　P. pressing service

Q. motel　　　　　　　　　　　　R. luggage and deposit office

Examples

（A）迷你酒吧　　　　（L）季节性

① (　　)康乐部　　　　　　　(　　)24 小时送餐服务
② (　　)叫醒服务　　　　　　(　　)行李和贵重物品寄存处
③ (　　)多功能厅　　　　　　(　　)通风的房间
④ (　　)汽车旅馆　　　　　　(　　)团队协调员
⑤ (　　)青年招待所　　　　　(　　)商务中心 24 小时营业
⑥ (　　)保险箱　　　　　　　(　　)机场接送

2. Reading practice.

Discover the Eden Resort and Enjoy the Southern Sichuan Bamboo Sea

The Eden Resort Hotel covers an area of 300 mu. Its bamboo extension reaches dozens of kilometers from the hotel. The hotel is located in Yibin in southern Sichuan. Yibin is home to Wuliangye, the most famous wine in China. It has been blessed as the first city on the Yangtze River. It also boasts the Southern Sichuan Sea of Bamboo and the Xingwen Stone Sea, both national scenic spots. The hotel has all sorts of facilities with its recreational equipment particularly enjoyable. It has a 5,000 m^2 water-curing center, a yacht club covering a water area of 300,000 m^2 and a golf driving range—the first one in southern Sichuan, as well as a mountain-and-lake surrounding sightseeing area. Its guest rooms, villas, presidential suites, Chinese food, Western food, and the international conference center provide first choice for high-end conferences.

The special architecture formed like the shape of a bamboo shoot serves as the reception hall. Its two wings include guest rooms, conference rooms, recreation facilities and fitness gyms. The guest rooms have many standard suites, single rooms and suites with many classes: high grade, deluxe and administrative suites. The guest rooms, plus resort villas, commercial villas and presidential suites, add up to a total of 454 rooms (suites).

(1) Read the passage and decide whether the statements are true (T) or false (F).

① The Eden Resort Hotel boasts the national scenic spots of Western Sichuan Sea of Bamboo and the Xingwen Stone Sea.

② The Eden Resort Hotel has a variety of recreational equipment.

③ The reception lobby is the building formed like the shape of a bamboo.

④ The golf driving range is the first mountain-and-lake surrounding sightseeing area in southern Sichuan.

(2) Discussion.

If you are the guide of a group of overseas tourists, and you are going to stay at the Eden Resort Hotel, on the way to the hotel, some of the tourists ask about the hotel you are going to check in, how will you introduce the hotel to the tourists? And which aspect of the hotel will you focus on?

3. Complete the following dialogue.

(G=the guide　　T=the tourist).

T: Excuse me, where can we have a swim?

G: ①_____. （在一楼有室内游泳池） You can relax yourself.

T: Is there a recreation center?

G: Yes, it is on the second floor. There you can ②_____. （打棒球和保龄球等）

T: ③_____? （这里有美容院和纪念品商店吗？）

G: Wait a minute. I will get you ④_____. （一本酒店宣传册）

T: I need to check my e-mail. Is there an ⑤_____ （网吧） near here?

G: Certainly, madam. The business center at the hotel has ⑥_____ _____. （网络链接）

4. Simulation.

A tour group checked in Sheraton Hotel. A guest would like to know the recreational facilities in the hotel. Suppose you are the local guide, how will you introduce to the tourist about the recreational facilities?

Task 3　Wake-up Call

◇**Lead-in**

Due to the next day's close schedule, everybody in the group needs to get up early, so when the first day's itinerary ends up, Simon proposes that they should go to bed early. What's more, in order to ensure the second day's schedule, he specially asked the hotel for the wake-up call service, but he is till ready to wake them up by himself in the next morning in case of emergency.

◇**Analyzing the Task**

A wake-up call (also called alarm call in the UK) is a service provided by most hotels to provide a service similar to alarm clocks via a telephone. Wake-up service is generally divided into two kinds: automatic wake-up call and artificial wake-up call. Wake-up service is an important service of the hotel to the guests to facilitate the guests do better scheduling, therefore, the tour guide should ask the hotel for the wake-up call service. And if there's any problem in the hotel's wake-up call service, the tour guide should know beforehand, and handle it timely, so as to ensure the normal schedule.

The on-the-spot communication is as following.

(S: Simon　　G: the guest)

G: Will you do me a favor, Simon?

S: Certainly, sir.

G: This is my first visit to China. I wonder if I can ask for the morning call service.

S: Yes, sir. Anyone in our group can ask for the service. Would you like a morning call?

G: Yes, I must get up earlier tomorrow. I want to go to the Bund to enjoy the morning scenery there. You know this is my first visit to Shanghai. People say there is a marvelous view of a poetic yet bustling life at the Bund just at dawn.

S: That's true. At what time do you want me to call you up, sir?

G: At 6 sharp tomorrow morning, please.

S: What kind of call would you like, by phone or by knocking at the door?

G: By phone. I don't want to disturb my neighbors.

S: Yes, sir. I'll tell the operator to call you up at 6 tomorrow morning. Anything else I can do for you?

G: No. Thanks. Good night.

S: Good night, sir. Sleep well and have a pleasant dream.

◇ Developing Tasks

1. Match the words in Column A with the English equivalents in Column B.

Column A   Column B

a. distribute   A. buildings or rooms where people live or stay

b. facilitate   B. to supply something, or provide somebody with something

c. furnish   C. to make something easy or easier to do

d. accommodation   D. to decide or settle something conclusively

e. determine   E. consistent, conforming, or in agreement with something else

f. assemble   F. to divide something into shares and give the shares to a number of people

g. artificial   G. consisting of many different parts or people

h. dominant   H. more important, effective, or prominent than others

i. corresponding   I. gather together or come together

j. diversified   J. made by human beings rather than occurring naturally

2. Simulation.

Make a wake-up call based on the situation given below and act them out in class.

You are the guide from CTS. One of your tourists, Ms. Lin, wants to get up early for jogging in the morning. She needs twice wake-up call service. The first time is at 6:45 and the second time is at 6:55. Pay attention to the telephone manner.

3. Writing.

Write a passage to describe one hotel you have lived in or you want to live in, including the location, characteristics, and the reason why you like it. No less than 100 words.

Related Knowledge

1. The types of hotel.

In the world, there are various kinds of hotels. Hotel patterns are also becoming more and more diversified and fancy. In order to meet the needs of all kinds of passengers and meet the needs of the hotel's profitability, all sorts of new hotels are appearing.

According to the use of the hotel, hotels can be classified into 4 categories. The first is the merchant hotel. This type of hotel is given priority to business guests, and is always located at the commercial center (urban area), and offers guests comfortable accommodation, eating condition and recreational facilities, in addition, it also offers direct dial telephone, telegraph, telex and other modern communication facilities as well as typing, shorthand, secretarial, and video, projection and other special services. Senior hotels should also have 24-hour room service and 24-hour laundry service etc.

The second is the tourist hotel. This kind of hotel mainly opens to tourists who stays temporarily, and is generally built near the tourist spots. To make the tourists satisfied mentally and materially, it provides not only fine eating and living facilities but also entertainment, health care, shopping and other service facilities.

The third is the resident hotel (apartments and villas) which caters to permanent guests. Besides the general facilities, this hotel adopts household structure which includes kitchen fittings, office equipment and children's playhouse, in order to make the guests fully enjoy the joy of family. Long-staying guests should sign a lease with the hotel. At the same time, there are also a significant number of resident hotels which receive guests who stay temporarily (merchant hotels and tourist hotels also have a part of permanent guests).

The last one is the resort hotel. This kind of hotel mainly receives guests who travel for enjoyment, and is usually located in the scenic spot area. Geographical environment is an important factor to a resort hotel, which is a leisure hub and provides guests recreational facilities. Its customs are greatly influenced by seasons.

2. The reception facilities.

Hotels often provide entertainment; rooms for meetings, banquets, or balls; shops of various kinds; commodious lobbies; and cafes, bars, and restaurants. Basic facilities determine a hotel's reception ability and the condition, and the standard and quantity of hotel facilities determines the grade of the hotel. But no matter which level the hotel is, the basic facilities should have the following several aspects.

(1) Reception facilities.

A hotel should be equipped with appropriate reception facilities, which include the front desk reception hall, the front desk (including the reception desk, the information desk and the cashier's desk), the business center, the valuables deposit office, the assistant manager reception desk, etc.

(2) Guest reception facilities.

The guest reception facilities of a hotel should have adapted to the scale and standard of the hotel, including single rooms, standard rooms, luxury suites, presidential suites, etc.

(3) Catering facilities.

Catering facilities refer to the required Chinese restaurant and Western restaurant adapted to the scale and standard of the hotel, including table-ware, cookers, furniture, kitchen appliances and various eating utensils and so on.

(4) Recreational facilities.

Corresponding recreational facilities as well as the necessary equipment and bar service should also be equipped. The bowling alley, billiard room, electronic game room, swimming pool, gymnasium, sauna center, massage room and all kinds of supporting facilities are all provided for the guests.

(5) Operation support facilities.

The operation support facilities of a hotel include: ①engineering support facilities, such as distribution facilities, air conditioning, refrigeration facilities and backup power generation facilities, supply and drainage facilities, hot water supply facilities, the laundry room and needed equipment; ② security facilities, such as the intercom, broadcasting, fire-fighting and corresponding equipment and so on; ③internal operating facilities, such as the staff canteen, the staff dormitory and the staff club, the staff locker room, etc.

3. Make a reservation.

(R=the receptionist   G=the guide)

R: Good afternoon. What can I do for you?

G: Good afternoon. I'm calling from China Travel Service. Is it possible for me to reserve a suite for my guests?

R: Certainly, can you give me your name please, sir?

G: Li Hua. L-I, H-U-A.

R: Thank you, Mr. Li. But by the way, how long will they stay here?

G: They'll stay here for a week.

R: I'm glad you choose our hotel.

G: How much is the suite, please?

R: Your suite is 480 yuan (RMB) per day.

G: Does that include service charge?

R: 480 yuan a day, service is not included.

G: Meals included?

R: Meals included.

G: What services come with that?

R: For four hundred and eighty yuan a day, you will have one bedroom with air-conditioning, a sitting room, a bathroom, a TV set, a computer, a telephone and a major international newspaper delivered to your room every day.

G: Do I have to pay in advance?

R: Yes, you may pay half of it. The account will be settled later.

G: On which floor is the suite?

R: We have reserved two rooms for you to choose. One is on the first floor, the other is on the thirteenth floor. Both of them have a bathroom and face to the south.

G: What's the difference between them?

R: The conditions and the prices are the same. No difference.

G: Which is quieter? The guest asks for quiet rooms. They want to have a good rest at night.

R: The thirteenth floor is very quiet. The room number is 1316.

G: I think I'll take the one on the thirteenth floor.

R: OK. And the arrival and departure dates?

G: I'm not sure about their arriving time because their flight has been delayed. But they will leave on October 7th.

R: Then we can only confirm a room from October 1st to October 7th. I'm afraid we won't be able to guarantee you the room before October 1st.

C: What if there isn't any room if they arrive before that day?

R: Don't worry, sir. We can either put you on a waiting list or find you a room in a nearby hotel.

　　G: Fine, thank you. Goodbye.

　　R: My pleasure.

　　4. Useful Sentences.

　　(1) Make & confirm reservations.

　◇ I'd like to book a room, please.

　◇ What kind of room would you like?

　◇ For which date? / For when?

　◇ In whose name was the reservation made?

　◇ May I have your name and phone number, please?

　◇ What time will you be arriving? / When will you arrive?

　◇ I'm sorry, but we're fully booked for those days.

　◇ Sorry, we're overbooked. But I can recommend you another hotel.

　◇ Do you prefer a front view or a rear view?

　◇ Can you keep the suite blocked for Mr. Hans?

　◇ We are looking forward to seeing you next Sunday.

　　(2) Check in.

　◇ May I help you? / What can I do for you?

　◇ Would you like to check in, sir?

　◇ I'd like to check in.

　◇ I'm always at your service.

　◇ Do you have a reservation?

　◇ Would you please fill in this registration form?

　◇ May I see your passport, please?

　◇ Could you please sign here?

　◇ The bellman will show you up to your room.

　◇ Our check-in time is 2 o'clock in the afternoon. Would you mind waiting until then?

　◇ I have made a reservation in the name of George Smith.

◇ Do you have any rooms available? / Do you have any vacancies?

◇ Can you give me a wake-up call in the morning?

(3) Check out.

◇ May I have your room key, please?

◇ Just a moment, please. We need several (3 or 5) minutes to check your room. / I need several minutes to draw up your bill for you. / I'll draw up your bill for you.

◇ Here is your bill. Your bill totals RMB 500 yuan. (The bill covers the room charge 398 yuan, the laundry service 25 yuan, and 77 yuan for the dinner in our Western restaurant).

◇ Please confirm/make sure and sign here.

◇ Would you like to check it?

◇ How would you like to make the payment?

◇ Here is your card and your receipt/invoice. Please keep it.

◇ Our bellman will take your baggage to the car.

◇ Wish you have a nice trip.

◇ We look forward to serving you again.

Module 7
Talking about the Itinerary

An itinerary is a detailed plan for a tour. It has detailed information of the route and the plan for the journey. It offers information not only on the arrangements for the journey but also the features of the tour. An itinerary should therefore be as informative as possible. At the same time, it should also be interesting and attractive, like promotional material. A complete itinerary consists of items such as the tour title, the day-by-day events, the destinations, and the duration. A tour title usually focuses on the length and the location of the tour, for example, "A Three-Day Tour to Changsha". Day-by-day events give more specific information about destinations, scenic sites, accommodations, means of transportation, as well as special events.

◇ Learning Objectives

Knowledge

① Know how to make an itinerary for tourists.

② Master the vocabulary and expressions about an itinerary.

Skills

① Be able to plan different tour itineraries for tourists.

② Be able to answer tourists' questions about tour itineraries.

③ Be able to handle changes in the itinerary.

Quality

① Strengthen service consciousness and confidence.

② Foster self-study ability, problem-solving ability.

Task 1 Discussing the Itinerary

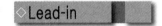

Simon is assigned to serve the tour group CITS20161008A. They will visit Changsha and Shaoshan from Oct. 8th to Oct. 10th. After good preparation, Simon has received the tour group successfully at Huanghua International Airport around 4:30 p.m. Now, the tour group has arrived at Sheraton Changsha. After dinner, Simon should discuss the itinerary with the tour leader.

Simon can successfully discuss the itinerary with the tour leader as following.

① Know exactly the scenic sites and the route.

Before planning an itinerary, Simon should know exactly the scenic sites. For example, in the first day, they will go to visit Yuelu Academy, Orange Island, the Museum of Hunan Province and the Xiang Embroidery Museum. When planning the itinerary, time should be considered.

② Discuss the itinerary with the tour leader as required.

a. Greeting.

b. Confirm the details of the itinerary.

c. Say goodbye.

The on-the-spot communication is as following.

(G＝the tour guide   L＝the tour leader)

(Simon knocks on the door of the tour leader's room in the hotel. He is going to talk with him about the itinerary.)

G: Good evening, sir.

L: Good evening, Simon. Sit down, please.

G: Thank you. Let's talk about the itinerary for this trip.

L: Fine. Our group received a copy of the itinerary from your travel service before we left for China. I'd like to know if there is any change.

G: Generally speaking, no. But still I think we should confirm some details of the itinerary, so everything will be well planned and everything can be made right.

L: That's right. OK, let's go over it again.

G: You will stay in Hunan for three days form April 20 to 22, and then pay a vist to Guilin.

L: Yes.

G: Today is April 20. There is no activities this evening, for the guests need a good rest after the long flight.

L: Good idea.

G: Tomorrow, April 21, we will have a full day to visit Changsha City, including Yuelu Academy, Orange Island, the Museum of Hunan Province and the Xiang Embroidery Museum.

L: And how about lunch and dinner?

G: Lunch is at Changsha Fire Palace Restaurant, which is a famous restaurant for local snacks. And dinner is at the Western restaurant of this hotel.

L: Good.

G: And the next day, April 22, we will go to visit the former residence of Chairman Mao, the Statue Square in the morning, and the Drop Water Tunnel in the afternoon, then back to Changsha. Lunch is at the restaurant of Maos and dinner is also at the Chinese restaurant of Sheraton, then you will be transferred to the airport for your departure flight to Guilin at 9:00 pm.

L: Yes, everything is clear, thank you. We'll leave everything up to you, then.

G: The itinerary covers so many places. I'm afraid you'll be exhausted.

L: Never mind. Everybody in this group is physically fit. Thank you for everything you've done for us. It's wonderful.

G: My pleasure. If there would be any changes, I'll let you know in time.

L: That's fine.

G: Thanks for your time. Goodbye and good rest, then.

◇ **Developing Tasks**

1. Listen and fill in the blanks.

(Simon, from CITS, is discussing the itinerary with the tour group leader, Mr. Black.)

(S=Simon   B=Mr. Black)

S: Good evening, Mr. Black.

B: Good evening, Simon.

S: I've come to discuss your ___①___. Can you ___②___ some time right now?

B: Sure. Our group ___③___ a copy of the itinerary before we came to China. Have there been any ___④___?

S: There have been no changes so far.

B: OK. Then let's ___⑤___ the itinerary. We stay in Beijing for seven days. Then we go on to Chongqing for three days. Our last ___⑥___ is Sichuan Province, where we stay for five days. The whole trip will last 15 days. Is that correct?

S: ___⑦___. If there are any changes, I'll let you know ___⑧___.

B: Oh, that'd be great. Then we'll leave everything to you.

S: My pleasure. If you or any of your group members need any help at all, don't ___⑨___ to ask. I hope you will have a ___⑩___ time in China.

B: Thank you.

2. Special terms.

(1) Put the following into English.

① 精选路线   ② 附加旅游项目

③ 自由活动时间   ④ 特别服务要求

⑤ 组团人数   ⑥ 民俗旅游

⑦ 行业考察旅游   ⑧ 路线图

⑨ 旅游者过夜数   ⑩ 延长逗留

(2) Put the following into Chinese.

① foreign escorted tour   ② final itinerary

③ full appointment   ④ best-selling China-tours

⑤ entertainment and diversions ⑥ on-shore visit

⑦ estimated time of arrival ⑧ travel arrangement

⑨ mini-destination area ⑩ sightseeing tour

3. Please fill in the blanks.

The tour group will spend a full day tour to Changsha City, including visiting Yuelu Academy, Orange Island, the Museum of Hunan Province and the Xiang Embroidery Museum. They will have lunch at Changsha Fire Palace Restaurant and dinner at Zan Feast Restaurant, Sheraton Changsha. Please fill in the blanks according to the given information.

Time	Place	Activity
8:00 a.m.—10:00 a.m.		Sightseeing
10:00 a.m.—12:00 p.m.		Sightseeing
12:00 p.m.—13:30 p.m.		Having lunch
13:30 p.m.—16:30 p.m.		Sightseeing
16:30 p.m.—18:00 p.m.		Sightseeing & shopping
19:00 p.m.—		Having dinner

4. Decide whether the following statements are true (T) or false (F).

(   ) A complete itinerary should consist of the tour title, day-by-day events, destinations and duration.

(   ) A tour title focuses on the location of the tour.

(   ) Day-by-day events give more specific information about the tour.

(   ) The accommodation and means of transportation should also be included in an itinerary.

5. Complete the following dialogue in English with the information given.

(A=the tour leader   B=the local guide)

A: It seems everything is settled. Shall we have a discussion about the itinerary, Mr. Li?

B: ①_____(当然). ②_____(这是我草拟的临时方案). ③_____(请看一看再告诉我您的意见).

A: Well, it seems that the itinerary is not suitable for the older tourists. ④_____(是不是一切都要缓慢而放松?)

A: Yes, they want to have a relaxing holiday.

B: ⑤_____（要不要我把叫早推迟到八点半？）

A: That would be nice.

B: ⑥_____, ⑦_____（如果起床晚了，可能没法参观计划里的某些地方）

A: That doesn't matter.

B: ⑧_____, ⑨_____（那他们对什么感兴趣，我们该减去什么节目？）

A: Don't worry about that. They have already given me a list of tourist attractions that they would like to see.

B: Good. ⑩_____（可以让我们看一看吗？）

A: Can you put these activities into the new itinerary?

B: (11)_____（这对我来说并不难）

A: Wonderful! They will appreciate it if you can meet their requests.

B: It's my pleasure. (12)_____（这是我的手机号码，如果你遇到困难，务必联系我）

A: Sure, thank you.

6. Simulation.

Suppose you are a travel agent, Mr. and Mrs. Brown want to have a tour in Shenzhen, Guangzhou and Zhuhai, please discuss the itinerary with them.

Task 2　Handling Changes in the Itinerary

◇Lead-in

Simon has discussed the itinerary with the tour leader, but the next day, when he informed the tourists of the itinerary, some of them have different ideas on the itinerary and want to make some change of it. How should Simon handle it?

◇Analyzing the Task

Simon can successfully handle the requirements of the tourists as following.

① Ask and understand the guests' special requirements.

Before planning an itinerary, Simon should talk with the tour leader to know better about what exactly the tourists want to see and he'd better plan the itinerary according to the information he got.

② Discuss the arrange of the new requirements in a professional manner.

The on-the-spot communication is as following.

(After breakfast, in the hall of the hotel, Simon is explaining the day's itinerary to the tour group.)

(S=Simon   T=the tourists)

S: Good morning, everybody.

T: Good morning.

S: Did you have a good sleep last night?

T: Yes, excellent.

S: That's great. I'm glad you got a good rest, as we have many activities for you to enjoy today.

T: What places are we going to see today?

S: You can check the itinerary you've received. As planned, we are going to four places in Changsha City, including Yuelu Academy, Orange Island, the Museum of Hunan Province and the Xiang Embroidery Museum. Yuelu Academy is our first stop. We will arrive there at 8:00 am, and then stay for two hours. And then we'll go to Orange Island, which is not far from Yuelu Academy and you can stay there for two hours. You can walk along the Xiangjiang River. Then at 12:00 am, we will meet at the place where you get off the bus and head to Changsha Fire Palace Restaurant for lunch. After lunch, at 13:30 pm, we'll go to visit the Museum of Hunan Province. I think you'd like to get more knowledge from it, so I leave you more time in it. Three hours later, we'll go the Xiang Embroidery Museum. Then at 7:00 pm, we'll be back at the hotel for dinner. Is that all clear to everyone?

T: Yes.

S: Do you have any questions about the itinerary?

T: Yes. I'd like to know if there is any plan during the night.

S: No, I think you'll be exhausted after the full day activity.

T: I heard that the fireworks in Orange Island is very famous, if possible, we want to have a look.

S: OK, if you want to see it, I'll try my best to meet your need. Any other special requirements?

T: Chinese tea is very popular and some of the tour members want to buy some. Can you arrange that?

S: No problem. I will take you to a tea shop on the way back from the tour tomorrow. Is that OK?

T: That's very kind of you.

S: If you have any other requirements, do let me know. I will try my best to make your trip pleasant.

T: Thank you.

S: OK. Now let's go on the bus. Our driver Mr. Li is waiting for us outside the hotel.

◇ **Developing Tasks**

1. Complete the following dialogue in English with the information given.

(A＝the local guide   B＝the tour leader)

A: Mr. Jones, ①_____（既然你已经办好入住手续,我们可否简单地讨论一下明后天的活动?）

B: Yes, of course. That's a good idea. When shall we start tomorrow morning?

A: ②_____（我准备九点出发,可以吗?）

B: Yes, that will be fine. Will we have a busy day tomorrow?

A: Not really. ③_____（作为一个南京本地人,我建议第一次去中山旅游区）④_____（上午参观中山陵和明孝陵）

B: That sounds very pleasant. I'm looking forward to it.

A: For the afternoon, we will tour the Linggu Temple. ⑤_____（傍晚我们可以去夫子庙漫步,并品尝秦淮小吃）

B: The Qinhuai snacks sound OK, but why visiting two temples? We have seen quite a few temples since we arrived in China.

A: You are right. ⑥_____（但我保证夫子庙是独一无二的）During the Ming dynasty, the temple served as a school for children of the imperial court. ⑦_____（与其他的佛教寺庙很不一样,绝对值得一游）

B: OK. We will do that then. Thank you for telling me this. Then what's planned for the day after tomorrow?

A: The next day can be spent by the Xuanwu Lake, passing by Taicheng, the Jiuhua Hill and the Jiming Hill. After lunch, you can go shopping in the Xinjiekou Commercial Circle. ⑧_____（新街口是中国第三大购物区，仅次于北京王府井和上海南京路）⑨_____（如果你们对中国的历史感兴趣，可换乘参观总统府）

B: This is a group of elderly people, most of whom are interested in history. We would very much like to see the former Office of President. Besides, we have had enough shopping in Shanghai.

A: OK, ⑩_____（那我们就不去购物了）

B: Thank you, that's very kind of you.

2. Simulation.

① Three students are to play the roles of the tour guide and Mr. and Mrs. Davis. They are discussing the following itinerary of a two-day tour in Shanghai.

Day 1, Morning: Jinmao Grand Tower and Shanghai Oriental Pearl Tower

Afternoon: Fudan University

Day 2, Morning: Yuyuan Garden

Afternoon: A visit to a local family

② A group of American tourists headed by Mr. Brown arrives in Hangzhou in March. They will stay in Hangzhou for two days. Miss Li, the local guide is discussing the itinerary with Mr. Brown. The tentative schedule is that Miss Li drafted a visit to the tea museum, while Mr. Brown insists on visiting a tea plantation instead. They are trying to reach an agreement to achieve mutual satisfaction.

③ Two students are to play the roles of Mr. Zhu, the local guide, and Mr. Jackson, the tour leader. Mr. Zhu has pressed a preliminary there-day sightseeing schedule for the group during their stay in Beijing. He is now explaining and discussing it with Mr. Jackson, who seems to be quite satisfied with the arrangement.

3. Translation.

① 在旅游团抵达之前的地陪应该仔细研究接团计划，并了解客人的情况，以便制定初步的行程安排。

② 导游应该本着"游客至上"的原则，切忌将自己的主观意见强加给别人。

4. Read the text through and then finish the task.

Designing Travel Programs

An itinerary is a detailed plan for a tour. It has the detailed information of the route and the plan for the journey. It offers information not only on the arrangements for the journey but also the features of the tour. An itinerary should therefore be as informative as possible. At the same time, it should also be interesting and attractive, like promotional material. A complete itinerary consists of items such as a tour title, day-by-day events, destinations, and duration. A tour title usually focuses on the length and the location of the tour, for example, "A Three-Day Tour to Xi'an". Day-by-day events give more specific information about destinations, scenic sites, accommodation, means of transportation, as well as special events.

The following is an example of "A Four-Day Tour to Shanxi".

Destinations: Mount Wutai, Yungang Grottoes, Pingyao Ancient City

Day1-Oct. 22(Mon.): Taiyuan

Day2-Oct. 23(Tue.): Mount Wutai

Day3-Oct. 24(Wed.): Yungang Grottoes

Day4-Oct. 25(Thu.): Pingyao Ancient City

Hotel: 3-star

Maximum group size: 15

Price: 3,800 yuan/person

The price includes:

Three night's hotel accommodation

Fights

Sightseeing as specified (excluding entrance fees)

Three breakfasts, four lunches, three dinners

Local English-speaking guides

Fill in the blanks.

① An itinerary offers information on both the arrangements for the journey and the _____ of the tour.

② An itinerary should be as _____ as possible.

③ A tour title usually focuses on the length and the _____ of the tour.

④ _____ give more specific information about the tour.

⑤ Find some information about a scenic site in your city and plan a three-day tour.

Day 1: _____

Day 2: _____

Day 3: _____

5. Listen and fill in the blanks.

To plan a perfect __①__ , you should keep in mind such matters as cost, __②__ , and the __③__ of stay.

First, choose where you aim to go for your vacation.

Then __④__ your itinerary. Surf the Internet or read some books about __⑤__ sites, places to visit, and things to do. Make sure you book __⑥__ means of transportation for the right dates.

Write down all the possible sites and choose those that suit you best. Older travelers may prefer to visit __⑦__ sites, while young people may like to visit shopping centers.

Get the right clothing ready for your holiday. If you are going to somewhere hot you may need shorts and T-shirts, but if you are going to a colder place you need to pack __⑧__ and warm __⑨__ .

Once you have chosen where you wish to go, you can now decide how you are going to get around—by car, taxi, train, plane, bus, or boat.

After you have __⑩__ all the information, find a map of your __⑪__ to help you get around.

Write down all the information you have gathered __⑫__ you forget.

◇ Related Knowledge

1. The SOP of talking about the itinerary.

Time: It should be done on the day of the tour group arriving, before the tour begins.

Place: It depends. Usually the hotel lobby is a good choice. For the very important group, the meeting room in the hotel may be necessary sometimes.

Object: It depends on the tour group situation. For the ordinary group, please talk with the tour leader. If there is no tour leader, please talk with the important person of the group or all the tour members. For the very important group, you'd better talk with the leader and the responsible person of the group.

Principle: Guest first, service first; reasonable and possible; equal consultation

Solution:

① The local guide should report the matter to the travel service leadership and try his best to arrange it if their proposal is reasonable and feasible.

② If an extra charge must be made for the added item, he must let the guests know and must collect the money at the set price.

③ If it is difficult or impossible to meet the guests' demand, he must give them a clear explanation and patiently persuade them to follow the original program.

2. Special terms.

Discussing schedules

draft 草拟	regarding tourists as supreme 游客至上
tentative 暂定的	at your request 按照你的要求
preliminary 预备的	superb service 优质服务
settled/arranged 安排好的	bear the expense 承担费用
itinerary planning 行程安排	in the capacity of 以……身份
means of traffic 交通工具	privilege 特权
abide by 遵守	mutual equality 相互平等

Activities involved

sightseeing trip 观光旅游	imperial garden 皇家园林
package tour 包价旅游	monastery/temple 寺庙
city tour 城市游	sightseeing guide book 观光手册
special interest tour 特殊兴趣游	set out/set off 出发
optional tour 选择性旅游	put off 推迟
place of interest 旅游景点	cruise 乘船游览
special event 特殊活动	head for 前往
day-to-day event 每日活动	be worth visiting 值得一游
scenic spot 风景点	recommend 推荐
theme park 主题公园	snack 小吃

historic spot 历史名胜   transfer 换车

ethnic minority and culture tour 少数民族风情游

3. Useful sentences.

(1) Start discussion on the itinerary.

◇ Shall we have a discussion on the itinerary?

◇ Let me say a few words about your itinerary.

◇ I've come to talk about the itinerary for your trip.

◇ May I give a brief introduction to the activities for the coming few days?

◇ I'd like to take a couple of minutes to familiarize you with the details of our journey.

◇ It's just a matter of the schedule, if it is convenient for you right now.

(2) Inquire what the foreign guest would like to see.

◇ Have you got any thing special in mind that you would like to see?

◇ This is the tentative plan I've worked out. Would you please go over the details?

◇ Are there any special places in which you are interested?

◇ We'll follow the itinerary we sent you the last time.

(3) Make suggestions about place to visit.

◇ Perhaps you would like to visit...?

◇ You might like to visit...

◇ It might be good idea to visit...

◇ I think you will find... interesting.

◇ We have a number of places that are worth visiting.

◇ For the afternoon, we will tour...

◇ The Great Wall is a must for all visitors to China.

◇ This restaurant is a must for anyone who loves Sichuan food.

(4) Make suggestions about the procedures.

◇ We should probably visit... first, and then go shopping if we are not pressed for time.

(We will leave everything up to you.)

◇ Why not visit a few more places of interest before lunch and find a fast-food restaurant instead of this one?

(It's all up to you.)

◇ I think we'd better make it 10:30, in case we get caught in the traffic.

(We will put everything completely in your hands.)

◇ Wouldn't it be better to reduce the shopping time to just one hour?

(5) Solicit opinions.

◇ What would you suggest instead?

◇ What would you suggest for the whole itinerary?

◇ What would you suggest for the schedule?

(I wonder if it is possible to arrange shopping for us.)

◇ What would you suggest for the arrangements?

(I can't say for certain off-hand.)

◇ Please read/check it to see if there is a need of any change.

(I can see you have put a lot of time into it.)

◇ If he wants to make some minor changes, we can try to arrange them.

◇ If you have any questions on the details, please feel free to ask.

Module 8
At the Restaurant

At the very beginning of restaurant service, the tour guide must be familiar with all the tourists. In other words, the tour guide shall know where the tourists come from and what tastes they like.

Generally speaking, the whole process at the restaurant includes contacting with the restaurant, booking tables, introducing the menu, teaching the tourists some expressions and culture in different kinds of restaurants, such as dining at a Chinese restaurant, at a Western restaurant or tasting local food. You also tell everyone the precise time and place of dining, and lead them to the right dining room.

◇ Learning Objectives

Knowledge

① Know the work process about treating guests at the restaurant.

② Master the vocabulary and expressions about restaurants.

Skills

① Be able to teach the guests some easy expressions at the Chinese restaurant and the Western restaurant.

② Be able to check the different tastes of the guests.

③ Be able to book tables in advance.

④ Be able to lead the guests to enjoy the local food and snacks.

Quality

① Prepare all the preparations in advance.

② Strengthen problem-solving ability and interpersonal communication and coordination ability.

Task 1　Booking Tables

◇Lead-in

Simon, a local guide from Changsha, has arranged all the tourists to have a rest after a long journey. It is time to book tables for them. Simon has got touch with some different restaurants in advance. Now he's calling one of the restaurants. What shall Simon say at this moment?

◇Analyzing the Task

Simon must do as following.

① Give the receptionist the precise number of the people.

② Inquire the menus.

③ Tell the time of arriving at the restaurant.

The on-the-spot communication is as following.

(L＝the local guide　　W＝the waiter)

W: Hello, this is Century Restaurant. Good afternoon. May I help you?

L: Hello, this is Simon from CITS. I want to book some tables for twenty-one people to have dinner this evening.

W: OK, I see. What kinds of tastes do the tourists like?

L: They are all from England, so they want to taste Changsha cuisine.

W: OK! What's the time of your arrival, please?

L: About 6 o'clock.

W: OK! We hope you can pay 20% of the total as a deposit.

L: No problem.

W: We'll keep your tables until 8:15 p. m.

L: OK. Could you give us some tables by the window?

W: Certainly. Thank you for calling, sir. We look forward to your visit.

◇Developing Tasks

1. Matching.

① ② ③

④ ⑤ ⑥

A. menu   B. dining room   C. telephone

D. receptionist   E. waiter   F. drink list

2. Phrases interpreting.

准确人数		一行 21 人	
餐馆前台		餐桌预订	
旅行社		菜单	
到达时间		提前	

3. Discuss and write down.

When you book tables, what precautions should you care about?

_____
_____
_____
_____

4. Listen and fill in the blanks.

A waiter is receiving a telephone call from a local guide to book tables for tonight.

(G＝the guide   W＝the waiter)

W: Good morning. Century Restaurant. ① _____ ?

G: I'd like to ② _____ , please.

W: ③ _____ ?

G: Around 7:00 p.m.

W: I'm sorry sir, we are ④ _____ for 7:00, but would you mind some waiting?

G: ⑤ _____ ?

W: Eight o'clock should be OK.

G: OK, please ⑥ _____ it at eight.

W: ⑦ _____ ?

G: Steven. By the way, we'd like a table ⑧ _____ .

W: ⑨ _____ , Mr. Brown. We're ⑩ _____ to having you with us tonight. Thank you for calling.

G: Goodbye!

W: Goodbye!

5. Simulation.

Simon, the local guide from CITS, is booking tables for a tour group of 20 members from England at Century Hotel. The tour leader is James Brown. The tourists' arrival time is 6 p.m. He will accompany them to the restaurant for dinner.

Task 2   Dining at a Chinese Restaurant

◇Lead-in

People in different countries have different ways of cooking, serving and eating, as a tour guide, he/she is asked to have some knowledge of Chinese cuisine, in order to introduce the local cuisine well and help the guests to choose food. Simon, a local guide, is leading a tour group to dinner in a Chinese restaurant. How should Simon explain the food and help the group to order?

◇Analyzing the Task

Simon can do the task as following.

① Be familiar with Chinese cuisine and local food.

② Anticipate and understand the guests' needs by asking right questions, listening, communicate with F&B attendant effectively.

The on-the-spot communication is as following.

(S=Simon   W=the waiter   T1= Tourist 1   T2= Tourist 2)

W: Hello. Welcome to our restaurant. May I help you?

S: Yes. Our travel agency has booked some tables for twenty-one people to have dinner this evening.

W: I see. Please follow me.

S: Thank you.

S: Ladies and gentlemen, here we are in Century Restaurant. This is the coat rack. You can leave your coats here.

T1: That's great.

W: May I have your order now? This is the menu.

S: We'd like some of your local specialties.

W: I recommend Steamed Fish Head with Chopped Peppers, Dong'an Chicken and Braised Pork with Mao's Family Style. These dishes are unique in Hunan, a little spicy, but tender and pleasant to the plate.

T2: These all sound good. We'll take that. What tofu specials do you have?

W: We can offer you Mapo Tofu and Stinky Tofu.

L: Sticky Tofu smells rotten but tastes really good, and it is special and popular in Changsha. Mapo Tofu is a typical food of Chuan cuisine. It is flavorful and a little spicy.

T1: I like Mapo Tofu.

W: What vegetables would you like?

S: Spinach with garlic sauce, and mushroom soup.

W: What would you like to drink?

S: Twenty-one glasses of orange juice, please.

W: So, your order is Steamed Fish Head with Chopped Peppers, Dong'an Chicken and Braised Pork with Mao's Family Style, Mapo Tofu, mushroom soup, and twenty-one glasses of orange juice.

S: Exactly.

W: Your meal will be served right away.

◇Developing Tasks

1. Matching.

① ②
③ ④

A. mushroom   B. orange juice

C. pork with salted vegetable   D. private room

2. Discuss and write down.

What are the table manners in a Chinese restaurant?

_____
_____
_____
_____

3. Discuss and make a dialogue.

When you lead foreign guests to a Chinese restaurant for the first time, how to introduce to them? Try to make a dialogue about it.

_____
_____

_____

_____

_____

4. Listen and fill in the blanks.

A waiter is serving two visitors in a Chinese restaurant

Waiter: I'm sorry for ① _____. This is the menu. Are you ready to order now?

Tom: Sorry, we haven't decided yet. ② _____?

Waiter: No problem.

Tom: Well, I think I would like to ③ _____. How about you, Jones.

Jones: The same for me, please.

Waiter: Yes, sir.

Jones: What ④ _____ would you like, Tom?

Tom: Well, I'd like ⑤ _____, please.

Jones: I'll have ⑥ _____.

Waiter: Would you like a dessert?

Jones: ⑦ _____?

Waiter: Lemon pie, hot cake in syrup, chocolate.

Tom: Well, I think we'll order after we finish the main courses.

Waiter: All right, I'll bring ⑧ _____ right away.

5. Simulation.

Steven, the local guide from Changsha, is leading some tourists to a Chinese restaurant: Century Restaurant. Steven booked some tables and ordered some specialties.

Task 3　Dining at a Western restaurant

All the tourists are from England, so as a tour guide, Simon, recommends a Western restaurant to the tourists. It's half past six now and all the tourists are in the restaurant. What are the table manners in Western restaurants?

◇ Analyzing the Task

Simon can do the task as following.

① Be familiar with the Western restaurant.

② Help the guests choose food and communicate with the waiter carefully.

The on-the-spot communication is as following.

(S: Simon   W: the waiter   Ts: the tourists)

W: Good evening. Welcome to our restaurant. May I help you?

S: Yes. Our travel agency has booked some tables for twenty-one people to have dinner this evening.

W: OK. This way, please. (The tourists follow Steven)

S: Thank you very much.

W: Here is the menu. May I take your order?

S: Thanks, but I have to talk with my tourists about it. Could you wait us a little longer?

W: Yes, take your time, please.

S: Everybody, how about tasting an appetizer, tomato soup?

Ts: OK, that's good.

S: And what main course would you recommend?

W: Our steak is very good. It's the chef's recommendation.

S: OK, then, twenty-one steak.

W: What would you like to go with your steak?

Ts: Carrots and french fries, onions and fried eggs.

W: Anything to drink?

S: Red wine.

W: When will you order your dessert?

S: Maybe after our main course.

W: You have ordered tomato soup, steak with carrots and French fries, steak with onions and fried eggs, red wine. We will serve your meals quickly. Just a moment.

◇ Developing Tasks

1. Matching.

① ②
③ ④

A. tomato soup   B. knife and fork   C. steak   D. red wine

2. Discuss and write down.

What are the table manners in Western restaurants?

_____
_____
_____
_____

3. Discuss and make a dialogue.

Jack and Jim are deciding what to have for their meal. Try to make a dialogue about that.

_____
_____
_____
_____

4. Listen and fill in the blanks.

A waiter is serving five visitors.

(V=the visitor   W=the waiter)

W: ① _____, sir?

V: I'd like a table for five.

W: ② _____?

V: Oh, I'm afraid not.

W: Well, this way, please. ③ _____?

V: Yes. I'd like ④ _____.

W: ⑤ _____, sir?

V: Well done, please.

W: Your order will be ready in 10 minutes.

V: Thank you.

5. Simulation.

Simon, as a local guide from Changsha, is in a Western restaurant with some tourists. Steven is communicate with the waiter and talk with his tourists about the course.

Task 4　Tasting Local Food

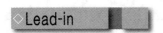

The Fire Palace is a typical place in Changsha which integrates folk culture, cooking culture and temple culture. Simon, as a local tour guide, is leading a tour group to the Fired Palace in Pozi Street. They arrived there at 5:30 pm. How should Simon recommend the local special food to the tourists?

Simon can do the task as following.

① Be familiar with the local food and the restaurant.

② Help the guests choose food and communicate with the waiter carefully.

The on-the-spot communication is as following.

(S=Simon   W=the waiter   Ts=the tourists)

S: Good evening, everyone. Here is Pozi Street, Changsha. There is a local restaurant gathering most famous local snacks in Changsha, which is the Fired Palace.

Ts: Great. We are so luck to taste the local snacks.

S: OK. Let's go into the restaurant. (The tourists follow Simon)

W: Hello. Welcome to our restaurant. May I help you?

S: Yes. We all want to taste some delicious local food.

W: I see. Please follow me.

S: Thank you. (After the tourists are seated)

W: Here is the menu. May I take your order?

S: Sure. We want some local food.

W: I recommend Sugar Oil Baba made of glutinous rice, Stinky Tofu, Tasty Shrimps made of shrimps and hot peppers, Steamed Fish Head with Diced Hot Red Peppers, Dragon Fat and Pig Blood, Fried Pork with Green Peppers and meat ball soup. These are all local food, which will be delicious for you.

S: That sounds good. We'll take these. Other suggestions?

W: Sisters Steamed Stuffed Buns, soybean-flour cakes.

S: OK, give us some.

W: So, your order is Sugar Oil Baba, Stinky Tofu, Tasty Shrimps, Steamed Fish Head with Diced Hot Red Peppers, Sisters Steamed Stuffed Buns, soybean-flour cakes. Is that all?

S: Exactly.

W: Your meal will be served right away.

◇ Developing Tasks

1. Matching.

① ② ③

④　　　　　　　　　　⑤　　　　　　　　　　⑥

A. Sugar Oil Baba　　　　　　　　　　B. soybean-flour cakes

C. Steamed Fish Head with Diced Hot Red Peppers　　D. Stinky Tofu

E. Sisters Steamed Stuffed Buns　　　　　F. Tasty Shrimps

2. Discuss and write down.

Make a five-minute speech to introduce Changsha local food.

_____
_____
_____
_____

3. Make a comment.

If it is the first time for you to taste Changsha local food, what comment will you make?

_____
_____
_____
_____

4. Listen and fill in the blanks.

Snacks, snacks and more snacks. There are ___①___ to choose from and most of them ___②___ and they are for tourists to bring home. I've just been out shopping and OK, here is a tip, well, I just learned that parched rice is very famous in Hunan Province. If you are looking for something for ___③___, it is a good idea to get some. In fact, it is processed by ___④___, and is ___⑤___.

5. Simulation.

Steven, a local guide from Changsha, leads his tourists to a local restaurant—the

Fired Palace. Steven orders some famous local cuisine, and it's the first time for the tourists to taste Changsha food.

◇ Related Knowledge

1. The qualifications for being a good tour guide in the restaurant.

① Try to tell your tourists why you would like to choose these restaurants.

② As a tour guide, it is quite often that you introduce the local cuisine to the guests. Also, you have to introduce some table manners to your group.

People in different countries have different ways of cooking, serving and eating. The British and Americans like to eat raw vegetables and have their meat half-done. Usually, they cannot appreciate the Chinese way of picking dishes for their guests, which may be considered unsanitary.

2. Table manners at the Western-style dinner.

As a formal dinner, it is customary for the man to help the lady on his right to be seated (by standing behind her chair, pulling it out from behind for her, and helping her to pull it close to the table as she sits down).

During the meal, try to keep up some kind of small talk with your neighbors every now and then. Otherwise you may be considered impolite.

After you are seated, take the napkin from the table, unfold it, and spread it across your lap.

When serving yourself, take small portions. If you don't like some particular dish that is served or if you have had enough of it, it is permissible to refuse a serving when someone offers it to you.

You don't have to wait for the host or the hostess to start eating, but of course leaping at your food like a starved wolfhound will not look very nice.

When you are eating soup, the soup spoon is tipped slightly away from you and is filled by moving it away from you, not toward you. Avoid making a noise by hitting the spoon against the plate. Sip the soup from the side of the spoon or from the end, but do not make a sucking noise.

Hold the fork in the left hand. The prongs should curve down and serve to hold the meat firmly in place while the knife, held in the right hand, is used to cut the meat.

Some Americans cut up the whole serving of meat first. Then they put down the knife, switch the fork to their right hand and proceed to use the fork to lift the food into their mouths. However, this procedure is not considered correct in the UK. In the UK, the diner cuts the meat, as described above, and he uses the fork in the left hand to lift the food to the mouth, one piece at a time.

It is considered bad manners to smoke while eating.

Never hold the knife in the left hand (unless you are left-handed).

Wipe your mouth with your napkin, but never do so while holding a knife or fork.

3. Eight famous cuisines in China.

Chinese cuisine is an important part of Chinese culture. With a history of several thousand of years, it is one of the world's three largest kingdom of cuisine.

The diversity of geography, climate, customs and products leads to Eight Cuisines of China. They are Shandong, Huaiyang (Jiangsu), Sichuan, Guangdong, Zhejiang, Hunan, Fujian, Anhui. Each cuisine has its own typical characteristics.

Features of each regional cuisine

Sichuan and Hunan cuisines: hot spicy (numbing, sour)

Anhui and Fujian cuisines: inclusion of wild game from their mountains

Guangdong, Fujian, Zhejiang, Jiangsu cuisines: great seafood, and generally sweet and light flavor

Shandong cuisine: fresh and salty with a lot of seafood dishes

Some famous Chinese dishes

Lu cuisine: Braised Abalone, Sweet and Sour Carp, Dezhou Grilled Chicken

Huaiyang cuisine: Three Sets of Ducks, Lion's Head Braised with Crab-Powder

Chuan cuisine: Mapo Tofu, Kung Pao Chicken, Lamp-Shadow Beef, Lung Pieces by a Couple and Sichuan Hot Pots, Pork Shreds with Fishy Flavour

Guangdong cuisine: Roast Suckling Pig, Chrysanthemum Fish, Braised Snake Porridge

Zhe cuisine: Dongpo Pork, Beggar's Chicken, West Lake Fish in Vinegar, Shelled Shrimps Cooked in Longjing Tea, Sweet and Sour Pork Fillet

Hunan cuisine: Dong'an Chicken, Stew Fins, Diced Chicken with Dried Red Peppers, Fish Head Steamed with Chopped Chilis, Braised Pork, Spicy Shrimps

Fujian cuisine: Buddha Jumping over the Wall

Anhui cuisine: Braised Turtle with Ham, Fuliji Grilled Chicken

4. Useful sentences.

(1) Booking.

◇ I'm sorry we are booked out for this evening.

◇ When do you start to serve dinner in the evening?

◇ When is the restaurant open for breakfast?

◇ When are the restaurant hours?

◇ We'll keep your tables until 8:15 p.m.

◇ We have received many bookings and I cannot guarantee a table by the window.

◇ Thank you for calling, sir. We look forward to your visit.

(2) Dining.

◇ May I have your order now? This is the menu.

◇ These cuisines are tender and pleasant to the plate.

◇ What tofu specials do you have?

◇ What main course would you recommend?

◇ Our steak is very good. It's the chef's recommendation.

◇ Your meal will be served right away.

◇ We will serve your meals quickly. Just a moment.

Module 9
Visiting Scenic Spots

    For most people, almost any place can become a tourist destination as long as it is different from the place where the traveler usually lives. The large cities offer scenic attractions and cultural entertainment for all kinds of people with a variety of tastes.

    As a tour guide, he/she should make a good preparation before setting off, and on the way to the scenic spots, he/she has to give a brief introduction of the scenic spots to the tourists to help them get a general idea of it. During the process of visiting scenic spots, scenic spot explanation is most important. The tour guide should be very familiar with the scenic spots, and is ready to answer the questions which will be put forward by the tourists. After the sightseeing, the tour guide should count the number of the tourists and make a summary of the day sightseeing.

Learning Objectives

Knowledge

① Know the work process about service on sightseeing.

② Master the vocabulary and expressions of introducing scenic spots.

Skills

① Be able to ask for tourist information.

② Be able to introduce scenic spots.

③ Be able to introduce performances.

④ Be able to introduce folk-custom activities.

Quality

① Strengthen service consciousness and confidence.

② Foster self-study ability, problem-solving ability and presentation ability.

Task 1　City Sightseeing

Lead-in

Simon will take the tour group to visit the city of Changsha today. They will go to visit Yuelu Academy, Orange Island, the Museum of Hunan Province and the Xiang Embroidery Museum. What points should Simon pay attention to during the sightseeing service?

Analyzing the Task

Simon should do as following.

① Be familiar with the visiting route.

② Get more information about the tour group.

③ Give tour-guiding as required.

Ensure the language is vivid and strong.

Ensure the contents are concise and to the point.

Ensure the time and cost are within the limits.

Ensure the guests have a thorough enjoyment.

Ensure to combine explanation with guiding.

The on-the-spot communication is as following.

(S＝Simon　　T＝the tourist)

S: Good morning, ladies and gentlemen, welcome to Changsha City. Did you have a good trip?

T: Yes, we have a wonderful trip.

S: Good, glad to hear that. Now I believe that you're ready for the tour today.

T: Yes, we're dreaming of visiting the great Changsha.

S: Yes, Changsha is a very beautiful city. We call it a "star city". When we introduce Changsha City to our distinguished guests, we'd like to use the following four words: mountain, river, island and tower. Do you know what they mean?

T: No, could you tell us more about it? We're interested in it.

S: The mountain represents Yuelu Mountain; the river represents the Xiang River, our mother river; the island means Orange Island, it is the world's longest inland river isle, and the tower means the symbol of the ancient city of Changsha—the Tianxin Tower.

T: Wow, it sounds like a very wonderful city.

S: Yes, you're right. Although not an ancient capital city as Beijing, Changsha also has rich historical heritages including old wall remains, tomb sites, religious temples and buildings. What earn the city's reputation among tourists are two things. One is a great man in China's recent history, Chairman Mao Zedong and the other is Yuelu Academy, a time-honored academic school perched on the scenic Yuelu Mountain.

T: Oh, we know that. Mao Zedong, the greatest person in China.

S: Yes. And we will go to visit Shaoshan, his hometown, tomorrow.

T: Great. I can't wait. Let's set off.

S: OK. Follow me, please.

Developing Tasks

1. Special terms.

(1) Put the following into English.

① 水族馆   ② 传统文化

③ 自然美景   ④ 商业区

⑤ 工业园   ⑥ 高新技术开发区

⑦ 高速公路   ⑧ 立交桥

⑨ 地铁   ⑩ 儿童乐园

(2) Put the following into Chinese.

① Pearl River Delta   ② boulevard

③ municipal mansion   ④ tourist attraction

⑤ Special Economic Zone   ⑥ theme park

⑦ trading port   ⑧ infrastructure

⑨ seashore city　　　　　　　⑩ railway network

2. Complete the following dialogue.

(G＝the guide　　T＝the tourist)

(The tourists are at the gate of the Window of the World, a place of interest in Shenzhen)

G：①_____?（请等一会儿好吗?）I'll buy the tickets.

T：All right.

G：Here are your tickets. Please ②_____.（保管好）

T：Thank you.

G：Attention, please. Now it's 1:30 p.m., the time of sightseeing is 4 hours. ③_____.（我们 5:30 在门口集合）Is that OK?

T：Yes, that's OK.

G：Then, let's go in.

T：Why is it called the Window of the World?

G：④_____.（总体来说,它是世界历史之窗、世界文明之窗、世界旅游之窗）

T：How wonderful!

G：This is the World Square. ⑤_____.（这里是亚洲区,那边是美洲区）

T：That's great!

G：⑥_____?（今天玩得愉快吗?）

T：Yes, a great day I have!

3. Translate the following sentences into English.

① 汉正街小商品市场是中国中部地区最大的小商品集散地和批发市场,以其便宜的价格和极全的货物,每天都吸引着全国大量的商人、购物者和观光者。

② 历史上的武汉是"中国四大名镇"之一,商业网点流通渠道广,有"货到武汉活"之说。

③ 重庆的建筑依山而立,城市四周环山,因而赢得山城的美誉。

④ 武汉地处江汉平原东部,市区被长江和汉水分割成武昌、汉阳、汉口三镇。

4. Listen and fill in the blanks.

Wuhan, the ① of Hubei Province, ② of the cities of Wuchang, Hankou and Hanyang with a total ③ population of 10.91 million and an area of 8,494 square kilometers. As the largest city in ④ China and the ⑤ of land and water ⑥ on the middle ⑦ of the Yangtze River, Wuhan surely is the center of ⑧ , ⑨ , and ⑩ in Central China and one of the most important cities in China.

5. Simulation.

Two students are to play the roles of a local guide and a tourist. The guide is from China Comfort Travel of Guangxi. The tourist is from Switzerland. The guide is introducing the beautiful scenery of Guilin to the tourist, who is taking a cruise along the winding Lijiang River.

 Task 2 Cultural Landscape

Lead-in

Simon will take the tour group to visit Yuelu Academy. As one of the four most prestigious academies over the last 1,000 years in China, the academy has witnessed a history of more than one thousand years without a break, so it is called a "one-thousand-year-old academy".

Then how should Simon do to give a good sightseeing for the tourists?

Analyzing the Task

Simon must do as following.

① To have a thorough understanding and knowledge of the culture.

② Understand the tour group's needs and explain according to guests' interests.

③ Be familiar with the visiting route.

④ To understand the aesthetic characteristics of the cultural landscape.

⑤ Actively use appropriate guiding and explaining skills, ensure the popularity of the language.

The on-the-spot communication is as following.

(S=Simon   T=the tourist)

S: Good morning, ladies and gentlemen, as planned, today we're going to visit

Yuelu Academy. First, I'd like to know whether you know something about it.

T: Yes, I heard that Yuelu Academy is one of the four most prestigious academies over the last 1,000 years in China.

S: Wonderful, you're right. The academy witnessed a history of more than one thousand years without a break, so it is called a "one-thousand-year-old academy".

T: Anything more?

S: Of course. Have you ever heard the renowned "Huxiang School of Learning"?

T: A little. Can you tell us more about it?

S: Sure. It is right here that the renowned "Huxiang School of Learning" in the history of the li philosophy (the philosophy of principle) began to gain currency when Zhang Shi lectured in the academy in the Northern Song dynasty. And then Zhu Xi came here twice to give lectures. Later on, the academy saw other learning and ideas promulgated and exchanged such as Yangming School in the midst of the Ming dynasty, Donglin School in the last years of the Ming dynasty, Han School of the Qian Long and Jia Qing reigns and New Learning of the last years of the Qing dynasty. The academic learning and education system of Yuelu Academy have had a far-reaching impact on the formation and development of Hunan's cultural tradition.

T: Excellent! A wonderful history, a wonderful academy.

S: Yes, you're right. We're all proud of it. There is a quotation "The kingdom of Chu, the unique home of talents; the Academy of Yuelu, the very cradle of all", which acknowledges the greatness of Yuelu Academy, and points to the historical fact that Yuelu Academy has been considered by many the cradle of the great people of Hunan Province.

T: Wow, it has a long and wonderful history. So let's go inside and take a good look.

S: OK. Follow me, please.

◇ Developing Tasks

1. Special terms.

(1) Put the following into English.

① 故宫   ② 龙门石窟

③ 秦始皇兵马俑   ④ 乐山大佛

⑤ 布达拉宫   ⑥ 毛主席纪念堂

⑦ 文化遗产 ⑧ 天下第一关
⑨ 天坛 ⑩ 孔庙

(2) Put the following into Chinese.

① Arch of Triumph ② Notre Dame de Paris
③ Leaning Tower of Pisa ④ Statue of Liberty
⑤ Times Square ⑥ Pearl Harbor
⑦ Cape of Good Hope ⑧ Metropolitan Museum of Art
⑨ Regent Street ⑩ Niagara Fall

2. Complete the following dialogue.

(G＝the guide　T＝the tourist)

G：We're approaching Badaling and you'll see the Great Wall in a short while.

T1：Wonderful! We have been waiting so long for it.

T2：What's the length of the Great Wall?

G：① _____ (它长约 6 000 公里). That's why we call it in Chinese "Wan Li Changcheng".

T2：No wonder it's said that this wall is the only building that can be seen from the moon in outer space.

T1：What are those towers on the wall spaced at equal distances from each other?

G：They're ② _____. (烽火台) The Great Wall, you know, was constructed in ancient times to guard against invasion by nomadic tribes from the north. When people found enemy troops approaching, they would ③ _____. (从这个台上放烟火信号) When the guards in the neighboring tower saw the signals, they would do the same. In this manner, the signals would be relayed to the capital.

T2：What a striking idea these ancient Chinese had!

T1：④ _____? (那它有多高呢?)

G：The average height is about 7.5 meters. Now, we are here at the No. 4 Southern Tower, the summit of the Wall at Badaling.

G：Today, we're all great men because ⑤ _____. (俗话说"不到长城非好汉")

3. Translate the following sentences into English.

① 黄鹤楼底层大厅高10余米,厅内立巨幅壁画《白云黄鹤》,取材于仙人"橘皮画鹤"的故事。

② 古琴台,位于汉阳龟山西面脚下美丽的月湖之滨。人们熟知的"高山流水"的典故就源于此。

③ 出土于湖北省随州市的编钟被称为世界古代八大奇迹之一。

④ 都江堰位于成都西北57公里处是公元前250年修建的一项巨大水利工程。

⑤ 紫禁城占地175英亩,四周有护城河和城墙围护,城墙四周建有角楼。

4. Simulation.

Three students are to play the roles of a local guide from Hunan CITS and two tourists from Korea. They are at Zhangjiajie National Park. The guide is introducing the scenery to the tourists.

5. Listen and fill in the blanks.

____①____ is travel related with a country or a region's culture, especially the ____②____ of the local people, the history of the place, its art, ____③____, religion, and other ____④____ that have helped shape their way of life. Cultural tourism includes visiting urban areas, ____⑤____ historic or large cities and cultural ____⑥____ such as ____⑦____ and theaters. It also includes tourism to rural areas ____⑧____ the traditions of the local people including ____⑨____ and rituals, etc.

A tour guide should provide cultural, historical and other information to tourists. Before the trip, the tour guide should prepare an ____⑩____ to the destination, which includes the history, location, ____⑪____, its historical, national and international ____⑫____, etc. The guide should ____⑬____ the introduction ____⑭____ and interpret for visitors the cultural features of a location clearly and ____⑮____ during the trip.

Task 3　Natural Landscape

◇Lead-in

The tour group will go to visit Yuelu Academy in the morning. Since Yuelu Academy is at the foot of Mount Yuelu, the guests also want to know about Mount Yuelu. How should Simon introduce Mount Yuelu?

◇ **Analyzing the Task**

① Be familiar with the visiting route.

② Understand the tour group's interests.

③ Have an in-depth knowledge of natural sciences and related literary knowledge.

④ Understand the methods of enjoying the sight of nature landscape.

⑤ Actively use appropriate guiding and explaining skills.

The on-the-spot communication is as following.

(L=Linda　　S=Simon)

L: I want to know something about Yuelu Mountain. Could you give me some information?

S: Sure, my pleasure. Yuelu Mountain Scenic Area lies in the west bank of the Xiang River in Changsha. The whole Yuelu Mountain Scenic Area is well-known for its abundant scenic spots, including the Aiwan Pavilion, the Yuelu Mount Temple, the Yunlu Palace, the White Crane Spring, the Flying Stone and so forth. In addition, Yuelu Mountain is also an important site where many revolutionists ever met for the purpose of discussing important issues both at home and abroad.

L: I have heard about the Aiwan Pavilion, and it's from a famous poem.

S: Yes, you're right. The Aiwan Pavilion lies in the Qingfeng Gorge and was built in 1792 A.D. Its original name is the Red Leaf Pavilion and later according to the poem written by Du Mu, it was changed to the Aiwan Pavilion. I guess many of you are very familiar with the poem, of which the most famous verse is "Stop the carriage and watch the maple leaves until late; the leaves covered by frost are more red than the flowers in February."

L: So beautiful a poem. Anything more about it?

S: Yes, when talking about the Aiwan Pavilion, we can't forget our Chairman Mao. Mao Zedong once played and studied here in the course of his study period. Mao Zedong, in his youth, often invited his classmates, including Luo Xuekun, Zhang Kundi, to come to the Aiwan Pavilion so that they could express their opinions about the current situation while seeking truth of life. Because of this, when the pavilion was being rebuilt, Mao was later invited by Lida, President of Hunan University at that time, to inscribe the name of the pavilion, thus the characters on the tablet were written by Chairman Mao.

L: So cool. Wonderful. I can't wait to have a look at it.

S: Yes, it's worth visiting. If time permitted, you'd better go and visit it. If you need my service, I will be always with you.

L: You're so kind-hearted. Thank you very much.

◆ Developing Tasks

1. Listen and fill in the blanks.

The water before us is a part of the ___①___, called the ___②___. This lake is a must when you visit the ___③___. The wetland area for sightseeing accounts for two square kilometers, about 2 meters deep on average. I shall ___④___ the ___⑤___ of a wetland. A wetland is a area of ___⑥___ or ___⑦___. It is a water area that is ___⑧___ or ___⑨___ covered, for a short or long period of time, with ___⑩___, or ___⑪___, or ___⑫___; a wetland is also a small part of the sea area. Its depth of water does not exceed six meters at low tide. As you know, the wetland is considered the Cradle of Life and ___⑬___. Being ___⑭___ — ___⑮___, the wetland is a ___⑯___, ___⑰___, and it is also the ___⑱___. In 1971, the USA and other 36 countries signed ___⑲___ in Iran. China started to carry out items of the convention in an all-round way after 1994. On Dec. 12th, 2004, Xinghu Wetland Park, the first wetland park in China, was officially ___⑳___ in the convention. Attention to both sides of the lake. On the lake are more than 20 islands. ___㉑___ and ___㉒___ are two of them. This island before us is the biggest ___㉓___ for ___㉔___ in South China. As you know, red-crowned cranes are considered ___㉕___; there are more than 2,000 red-crowned cranes in the world, of which China ___㉖___ more than 1,000. This park, with 50 red-crowned cranes, ranks the 4th of this kind in China. This park is also a ___㉗___ for other rare birds.

2. Put the following Chinese into English.

① 出发前,地陪应至少提前十分钟到达集合地点等待。游客准点集合登车后,核实,清点实到人数。去景点途中导游应告知游客当日活动安排,提醒注意事项。

② 抵达景点时,下车前地陪要讲清并提醒游客记住旅游车的车号、停车地点及开车时间。进入景点后,在景点示意图前,地陪应讲明游览路线、所需时间、集合时间和地点等。游览中的导游讲解内容应繁简适度。

③ 具有良好心理素质的导游充满激情,乐观向上,机敏灵活,团结协作,彬彬有礼,公正无私。

④ 参观活动结束后返程途中,地陪要注意以下工作:回顾当天的活动,宣布次日的活动日程,提醒注意事项,安排叫早服务,确认早餐及出发时间等。

3. Simulation.

Form a group of two, one is the guide, the other is the tourist. Suppose that the guide is showing the tourist around a place of interest—the Wuhou Temple in Chengdu, please make a short dialogue.

◇Related Knowledge

1. Sightseeing guiding service.

(1) Prepare before setting off.

Prepare the reception program, tour guide flag/banner, loudspeaker, tour guide certificate, necessary tickets, cash, map, etc. Make sure the driver is ready, reconfirm the meals of the day, get to the appointment meeting place 10 minute earlier, count the tourists, and make sure no one is missing. Remind the tourists the weather, indoor or outdoor activities, dress, shoes, etc.

(2) Tour on the way.

Introduce the itinerary of the day, background information of the places to visit, recreational activities.

(3) Scenic spots guiding.

On arrival at the place to visit, before leaving the bus, remind again the bus number, parking lot, and the time to meet after the visit. Explain in detail in front of the tour map the best route to visit, how long to stay, when and where to meet. Confirm the time! Guide and explain during the tour. Pay attention to the emphasis of explanation and allocation of time. Make sure nobody gets lost.

(4) Visiting activities.

Prepare for interpreting for both the visitors and hosts.

(5) Return trip.

Summarize the day's activities, answer more questions, and make supplementary explanation. Announce the itinerary of the evening if there is any, or how long to stay in the hotel and when and where to meet the next day if there is no activities at night. Remind them to take their belongings.

2. Related special terms.

(1) Tourist attractions and resorts.

tourist destination 旅游目的地	tourist spot 旅游景点
tourist resort 旅游胜地	heritage site 名胜古迹
cultural heritage 文化遗产	eco-tourism 生态旅游

remains of ancient culture 文化遗址 remains of historic relics 历史遗址
national eco-park 国家生态公园 national geo-park 国家地质公园
national forest park 国家森林公园 game sanctuary 野生动物保护区
theme park 主题公园 amusement park 娱乐公园
botanical garden 植物园 holiday resort 度假胜地
holiday villa 度假村 summer resort 避暑胜地
ski resort 滑雪胜地 medical spring 疗养温泉
hot spring resort 温泉度假地 mountain resort 避暑山庄
national nature reserve 国家自然保护区
eco-agricultural garden for tourism 农业观光生态园
state-listed famous historic and cultural city 国家级历史文化名城

(2) Types of travelers/tourists.

tourist group 旅游团 package tourist 团队游客
individual tourist 散客 sightseer 观光客
regular tourist 回头客 excursionist 短途旅行者
overseas traveler 海外/出入境旅行者 day tripper 一日游游客
domestic traveler 国内游游客 veteran traveler 旅行家
cultural tourist 人文旅行者 nature lover 自然风光旅行者
eco-tourist 生态旅游者 travelling shopper 购物旅游者
business traveler 商务旅行者 coach traveler 包车旅游游客
train traveler 火车团旅游游客 self-drive traveler 自驾车游客
sea traveler 海上旅游游客 flight traveler 飞机团旅游游客
organized mass tourist 全包旅游游客 convention traveler 大会游客
meeting traveler 会议游客 independent traveler 自助游游客
exhibition traveler 展览/参展游客
MICE traveler (meetings, incentives, conventions and exhibition) 商务会展游客

3. Useful sentences.

(1) Before departure.

◇ Our coach is waiting outside.

◇ Here is the coach for our trip. Please keep the number in mind.

◇ Is everyone on the bus? The driver is ready to start the coach. (Yes, everyone is on the coach. I'm sure. We can go now)

◇ Shall we start our program for today now? (OK, we'll put ourselves completely in your hands)

◇ Please take your seats. We are leaving in just a few minutes.

◇ Let's start off now.

◇ All aboard, please!

◇ Please remember the number of our boat and come back here before 11 o'clock.

(2) On the way to a tourist attraction.

◇ After this, we'll drive on for about 40 minutes.

◇ As we go, I'll mention places of interest and talk about their history, cultural, or political importance.

◇ We're heading for the boat pier.

◇ We're approaching the Lingyin Temple; you will see the Lingyin Temple shortly. (Great!)

◇ It's going to be quite a day for you.

◇ We're going to take a boat cruise on the West Lake. The cruise will take about one hour and twenty minutes, including a visit to the biggest artificial islet named Lesser Yingzhou.

◇ I wish you all a pleasant time. Thank you.

(3) Opening speech.

◇ Hello everybody, my name is Mary. I am one of the two local guides that will accompany you on a conducted walk round the city today.

◇ Today I will show you around a well-known garden in China, Zhuozheng Garden.

(4) Introducing the scenic spots.

① Describing history.

◇ Today, we are going to tour the city of Hangzhou.

◇ Now, we are standing in front of the Tianxin Pavilion of the ancient Changsha.

◇ Shanghai has built a batch of landmark architectures that are known both at home and abroad. These buildings have become the new tour scenes in the city.

◇ Some place has a long history of... years.

◇ Some place is a... place/country with... history.

◇ Zhouzheng Garden was built in the Ming dynasty.

◇ There are many known historic sites around here.

◇ Nanjing is an ancient capital of dynasties in China's history.

◇ This temple has a long history dating back to the early period of the Tang dynasty.

◇ As an ancient Chinese saying goes...

◇ Just as there is paradise in heaven, there are Suzhou and Hangzhou on earth.

◇ I would like to compare the West Lake to Xi Shi, the ancient beauty. She looks charming whether richly adorned or plainly dressed.

② Natural characteristics.

◇ Some place is covered with...

◇ Some place is made up of/consists of...

◇ Guilin is renowned for its green hills, clear waters, fantastic caves and spectacular rocks.

③ Listing examples.

◇ There are many places of interest, such as...

◇ Some place has many places of interests, among which is...

④ Most famous for...

◇ Some place is famous/well-known for...

◇ Hong Kong is a shopper's paradise.

◇ Shanghai is truly a fascinating city often nicknamed as the Oriental Pearl.

◇ Hainan as the only tropical inland in China enjoys the clear sky, the azure blue sea, fresh air and beautiful scenery.

◇ With its agreeable climate, beautiful scenery and rich natural resources, it becomes one of the leading cities for a sightseeing tour.

◇ The Potala Palace has become the symbol of the splendid Tibetan culture for its magnificent and unique architectural style.

◇ The gourmet street encompasses services for catering, shopping and amusement.

◇ Tourists can experience the exotic atmosphere, taste the diverse foreign foods, purchase attractive souvenirs and enjoy a wide variety of recreational activities.

◇ Chengde is a famous summer resort.

◇ Yuanmingyuan is renowned throughout the world.

◇ Zhuozheng Garden is one of the top four classical gardens in China and was listed in the first batch of important historical sites under state protection.

◇ In 1990, Yellow Mountain was declared a World Natural and Cultural Heritage site by UNESCO Heritage Committee.

⑤ Pointing out interesting points during the tour.

In front of you is...

On your right / left you will see...

As we turn the corner here, you will see...

In the distance...

If you look up you will notice...

In a few minutes we'll be passing...

We are now coming up to...

You may have noticed...

Take a good look at...

I'd like to point out...

Module 10
Transportation

During the tour, tourists always have some free time. Tourists have to arrange the free travel by themselves. In a new place, it is important to use the public transportation to transport. The public transportation includes buses, taxis and subways. They are very convenient and cheap for tourists. On the other hand, tourists can rent a car if they have an international driving license. A car-rental trip is a popular way to travel nowadays. While in China, it is not possible to use foreign driving license. Foreigners should have a guarantor and pay a large deposit to rent a car. As a tour guide, you must let the tourists learn how to travel by public transportation and rent a car.

◇Learning Objectives

Knowledge

① Learn inquiring of the public transportation.

② Know how to take a bus, taxi and subway.

③ Know how to rent a car.

④ Master the vocabulary and expressions about transportation.

Skills

① Be able to take a bus, taxi and subway.

② Be able to rent a car.

Quality

① Be able to communicate with the local people.

② Be polite and patient to others.

③ Enhance communication ability.

Task 1　Public Transportation

◇Lead-in

The tour group always has free time for the tourists to have a free travel. Usually, the tour guide will tell the tourists how they could use public transportation and where they could take a bus or take a subway. Now, the tourists want to have a dinner at Huogongdian. Please help them to get there by bus, subway or taxi.

◇Analyzing the Task

Simon can do this task as following.

① Update the transportation information.

② Have a good knowledge of the transportation map.

③ Provide the guests with clear and accurate guidance.

The on-the-spot communication is as following.

(A=Susan　　B=Simon)

A: Excuse me. Could you tell me how to use the public transportation in Changsha?

B: No problem. Where would you like to go?

A: I'd like to go shopping with my students. Where should I go?

B: You can go to Wuyi Square. It is the city centre and you can go shopping and enjoy food there.

A: Oh, that sounds good. How can I get there?

B: There are three ways to get there, by bus, subway or taxi. You can take No. 201 bus. This bus runs from 6:00 to 22:00. It charges 2 yuan per person. The bus station is over there across the road. Besides, the subway is quite convenient. You can take Line No. 2 and take off at Wuyi Square station. It costs 4 yuan. Finally, if you come back late at night, you will take a taxi. It is about 15 yuan from Wuyi Square to our hotel.

A: The information is very useful. Thank you very much.

B: My job. Please be careful and pay attention to safety.

A: I will.

◇Developing Tasks

1. Translate the sentences from Chinese to English.

① 请在电影院下车。

② 这是给你的小费。

③ 你将换乘1号线。

④ 你能告诉我去天安门要怎么走吗?

⑤ 您能告诉我最近的地铁站吗?

2. Role play.

Situation One

Lily wants to go to Tian'anmen Square by bus. Please help her take No. 112 to get there. You must use the words below.

| get on | next to | six stops | ride | cheap |

Situation Two

A tourist asks you how to get to the Summer Palace. There are three ways to get three, by bus, by taxi and by subway. Please choose one and perform. You must use the words below.

| get to | transportation | transfer | convenient | fare |

3. Listen and fill in the blanks.

A: The plane will depart at __①__. Could you hurry up?

B: I'm not sure, because __②__. But I will try my best.

A: Well, __③__?

B: There is another way to the airport, but the distance is much more than this one. Do you mind to pay more?

A: No problem. I just worry about the time.

B: That's OK.

A: __④__?

B: OK. I'll go straight a little further.

A: Thank you. How much is it?

B: ⑤   .

A: OK. Here is 50 yuan.

B: Thank you. ⑥   .

A: Thank you.

B: ⑦   .

Task 2　Rent a Car

◇Lead-in

A lot of young tourists would like to rent a car during the journey. It's a popular and convenient way to travel. The tourists ask Simon to help them rent a car to Yueyang. Please help them complete the task.

◇Analyzing the Task

Simon can do the task as following.

① Maintain and update the car rental information.

② Provide a link between the guests and the car rental agency.

The on-the-spot communication is as following.

(T＝the tourist　　G＝Simon, the local tour guide　　S＝staff)

T: Hi, Simon. Could you do me a favor please?

G: Yes, what can I do for you?

T: I want to have a self tour to Yueyang. Could you help me rent a car?

G: OK. Have you ever rent a car before?

T: Yes, I used to rent cars in the UK.

G: That's OK. Please follow me to the rental agency with your driving license.

...

S: Good morning. What can I do for you?

G: Good morning. I want to rent a car. What kinds of cars do you have?

S: What size are you looking for? A compact, SUV or minivan?

G: How much are they?

S: A compact is about 150 RMB a day, a SUV is about 250 RMB a day and a minivan is about 300 RMB a day.

T: I'll take a compact.

S: We have Toyota, Volkswagen, Ford and Mercedes-Benz. Which one do you prefer?

T: How much is a Volkswagen Passat?

S: It's 200 RMB per day for automatic transmission.

T: OK. I will take that.

G: Is this price including insurance?

S: Yes. This price includes an insurance which covers everything.

G: How about mileage and gas?

S: You can have unlimited mileage for the car. But the gas is not included.

G: I see.

T: And must I return the car here?

S: Yes. You should return it here.

T: That's fine.

S: How long will you rent the car?

T: Just one day.

S: How many people will drive the car?

T: Just me.

S: When would you like the car?

T: 7:00 a.m. tomorrow morning.

S: OK. Please show me your international driving license and your guarantor's ID card.

B: I'm her guarantor. Here is my ID card.

T: Here is my driving license.

S: Thank you. Miss White, you have to pay 1,000 RMB as a deposit. Would you like to pay by cash or credit card?

T: By cash. Here is 1,000 yuan.

S: Thank you. Please have a look at the rental agreement. If there is no problem, please sign here.

T: Fine, no problem.

S: You can pick up your car from the parking lot on the first floor tomorrow morning with the rental agreement. The key is on the car. You have to return the car before 11:00 a.m. the day after tomorrow. As the gas is not included in the charge, you have to fill up the gas tank before you return. If not, we will charge you 10 RMB per liter.

T: OK. Thank you very much.

S: You're welcome.

◇ Developing Tasks

1. Please write down the correct words based on the sentences.

| pick up | insurance | key | SUV | driving license |

① — Do you have your _____?

— Sorry, I forget to take it.

② You can _____ the car now.

③ I want to buy the _____. I think it is necessary.

④ So you will take the _____ then, sir?

⑤ — Where is the _____?

— It's on the car.

2. Complete the conversation in English with the information given blow.

A tourist wants to rent a SUV from Oct. 11-Oct. 13. But he doesn't have a guarantor and he doesn't know how to gas up the car. The clerk helps him solve the problem. Please make a dialogue according to this situation. You must use the words below.

| rent | driving license | guarantor | deposit | liter |

3. Listen and fill in the blanks.

A: Good morning. How can I help you?

B: I want to rent a car.

A: We have ① _____ you can choose from. What kind of cars do you prefer, a compact or SUV?

B: I am here to travel with my girlfriend. I want her to have a good time.

A: Oh. You may have a Benz like this.

B: It must be very expensive. How about the price?

A: It's 50 yuan per day.

B: It's cheap! Does the price ② ?

A: Yes, of course.

B: But how can you do that?

A: Because this car ③ on it.

B: But it almost looks new. I like it.

A: So you will take the Benz then, sir.

B: Yes. I'd like to rent it ④ .

A: OK. May I have your ⑤ and ⑥ , please.

B: Here you are.

A: Thank you.

B: Where should I ⑦ ?

A: You have to return it here.

B: While in America we can ⑧ .

A: I'm sorry about that. But this car must be returned to this lot.

B: Never mind. Where is the key?

A: You have to first ⑨ and show me your ⑩ . And the key is on the car, you can take it when you pick the car tomorrow.

B: That's fine.

◇ Related Knowledge

1. Related special terms.

Volkswagen 大众

compact 小型车

driving license 驾照

Ford 福特

gas 汽油

automatic transmission 自动挡

deposit 押金

empty tank 空箱(汽油)

full tank 满箱(汽油)

guarantor 担保人

insurance 保险

manual transmission 手动挡

mileage 里程

pick up/drop off 取车/还车

rental agreement 租赁协议

TOYOTA 丰田

liter 升

Mercedes-Benz 奔驰

parking lot 停车场

car rental agency 租车公司

SUV 运动型多功能车

van 面包车

2. Useful sentences.

(1) Public transportation.

◇ Is it expensive to take the subway?

◇ I suggest you take the subway.

◇ You can take the taxi or metro.

◇ Turn left at the second corner.

◇ Where is the nearest bus stop?

◇ How can I get to the train station?

◇ Could you tell me how long it will take to get to the airport?

◇ It is not very far from the airport to the hotel.

◇ It's about 15 kilometers from the airport to the hotel.

◇ It will take about an hour from the airport to the hotel.

◇ It's about a fifty-minute ride from the airport to the hotel by the airport limousine.

◇ I want to take a bus to the cinema.

◇ It's easy to get there by subway.

◇ Is this the right subway to the city centre?

◇ How can I get out of the platform after I get off the train?

(2) Rent a car.

◇ How much is it to rent an economy car?

◇ Do you have an international driving license?

◇ I'd like to book a car for next Saturday.

◇ You have to pay 1,000 yuan as a deposit.

◇ How long would you keep this car?

◇ You have to show your guarantor's identity card.

◇ If you don't have a Chinese driving license, you can't drive this car.

3. Changsha transportation.

Changsha had convenient transportation even in ancient times, especially with more than one hundred watercourses, including the Xiang River and the Dongting Lake. Nowadays, Changsha enjoys national highways 107, 319 and 106, as well as several other speedways. Through Zhuzhou, the Beijing-Guangzhou railway connects with the Zhejiang-Jiangxi railway in the east and the Hunan-Guizhou railway in the west. The Shimen-Changsha provincial railway connects with the Yidu (Hubei)-Liuzhou (Guangxi) railway. Huanghua Airport is an international airport and has several international flight courses.

4. Changsha's airport.

Changsha Huanghua International Airport is 24.2 kilometers east to the center of Changsha City, near Huanghua Town of Changsha County. It is the biggest airport with the most complete establishment in Hunan Province. From Changsha Huanghua International Airport, there are non-stop flights to 53 cities including Beijing, Shanghai, Guangzhou, Shenzhen, Kunming and Chongqing.

5. Changsha's railway station.

The railway station is located at Dongzhanlu of downtown. It can be reached by many public buses such as 108, 110, 111 and 113. Changsha railway station is an important big modern station with different waiting halls for express trains and normal trains as well as honored guest waiting room. Everyday, there are nearly one hundred passenger trains departing or passing Changsha, reaching all the big and moderate cities of China. Since there is only one railway station in Changsha, it can at times be very busy.

Module 11
Shopping in Tourism

Shopping is one of the essential factors of tourism. Wherever they go, travelers will buy many daily necessaries before they set off. They will also buy many things needed during a tour, for example, cameras, travel bags, tourist guidebooks and so on. During the trip, people always do more shopping during their tour than the time staying at home. They will buy souvenirs for themselves and presents for their family and friends. Enjoyable experiences breed happy memories which are mental reminders of places, things and people. Therefore, a souvenir is something which helps bring back memories.

Statistically, about one half of the world's total spending on travel goes to shopping. Wherever they visit, tourists are likely to buy souvenirs in a local store to give as a gift or to remember their travel experience. They usually tend to seek the tour guide's advice as to what souvenirs to buy and where to buy them at a reasonable price. As a prospective tour guide, you are requested to recommend to your clients traditional local handicrafts or typical souvenirs with their unique features and exquisite workmanship. Your recommendation will help to stimulate their desire to buy things in a particular shopping arcade. But you have to make sure that any shoddy, vulgar and unreasonable goods are not sold to your guests at any time. Generally, shopping is an indispensable component of your travel arrangements. Excessive shopping arrangements, nevertheless, often cause dissatisfaction or even complaints on the part of tourists.

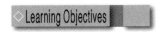
Learning Objectives

Knowledge

① Know how to introduce the local specialties to the tourists.

② Master the vocabulary and expressions about souvenirs, arts and crafts and tea.

Skills

① Be able to help tourists choose local specialties.

② Be able to recommend local specialties to tourists.

③ Be able to handle tourists' special needs.

④ Be able to give necessary reminding.

Quality

① Strengthen service consciousness and confidence.

② Foster self-study ability, problem-solving ability and presentation ability.

 ## Task 1　Souvenirs

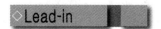

Simon is assigned to serve the tour group CITS20161008A which will visit Changsha and Shaoshan from Oct. 8th to Oct. 10th. After sightseeing, the tourists want to buy some souvenirs. As a tour guide, what should Simon know and what should Simon do?

◇Analyzing the Task

He can do as the following.

① Take the tourists seriously and have a positive attitude.

Each tour guide must be aware that meeting the demands/needs of the tourists is one of the important contents of tour guide service—to help tourists shopping is the responsibility of tour guides.

② Be familiar with the products.

In order to meet different tourists' requirements, a tour guide should understand the origin and quality of goods as much as possible.

③ Arrange appropriate shopping programs, offer guests with true and accurate product information, and give guests sincere suggestions.

The on-the-spot communication is as following.

(S＝the shopkeeper　　J＝John Smith　　G＝the tour guide)

S: Good morning, sir, can I help you?

G: Yes, our foreign friends heard that Chinese arts and crafts are famous for their workmanship. They'd like to take some home.

S: We have various kinds of articles, such as palm leaf fans, jade carvings, woodcarvings, bamboo carvings, lacquer ware, etc.

G: OK, we see. (Turn to John Smith) Smith, you can take a look.

J: (To the shopkeeper) OK, Miss, I want something typically Chinese and easy to carry.

S: Well, the tri-colored glazed pottery is beautiful, but it's fragile. Cloisonné is heavy and can be easily damaged. I suggest you buy some embroidery. It's easy to carry.

J: I'm interested in it. It looks so delicate.

S: Here is a piece of Su embroidery. It's hand-made in the technique of double-sided embroidery. Both sides display the exactly same pattern.

J: Let me see it. Oh, a dog's playing with balls. The dog is so cute. (Turn to the tour guide) What's your opinion, Simon?

G: I agree with you. It's so cute and kids will like it.

J: I'll take it.

S: What else do you want?

J: I like the cloisonné vase, but what a pity, it's inconvenient to carry.

S: If you are really interested, you can have it posted.

J: That's a good idea. Then I'll take this piece of embroidery and the vase. How much are they?

S: Five hundred in all.

J: Here is the money.

S: Thank you.

◇ Developing Tasks

1. Special terms.

(1) Put the following into English.

① 中国画　　　　　　　② 水彩画

③ 草书　　　　　　　　④ 文房四宝

⑤ 象牙雕　　　　　　　⑥ 唐三彩

⑦ 彩陶　　　　　　　　⑧ 景泰蓝花瓶

⑨ 檀香扇　　　　　　　⑩ 刺绣

(2) Put the following into Chinese.

① purple clay teapot　　　　② shell picture

③ snuff bottle　　　　　　　④ clay figure modeling

⑤ bodiless lacquer ware　　　⑥ glass-beaded embroidery

⑦ cross stitching　　　　　　⑧ Spring Festival couplet

⑨ charcoal drawing　　　　　⑩ genuine article

2. Complete the following dialogue.

(G＝the guide　　T＝the tourist　　S＝the saleslady)

T：Are there any department stores near our hotel? I want to do some shopping.

G：Yes. ①_____.（过几条街就有一个大百货公司）

T：Can you go with me?

G：Of course. （At the department store）

S：Good afternoon! Are you being served?

T：Good afternoon! I'm looking for a silk shirt for myself. Would you show me some, please?

S：Certainly. We have a wide selection of silk shirts here. ②_____ ____?（你穿多大尺码?）

T：About size 13.

S：③_____?（你喜欢这些吗?）

T：Oh, how nice! They all look beautiful. But the problem is that I'm not good at choosing.（Turning to the guide）④_____.（你能帮我吗?）

G：Yes, with pleasure.（Feeling his fingers over the shirts and then looking at the brand）

T：You're really a capable and versatile young man.

G：⑤_____.（谢谢你这么说）I can assure you that ⑥_____（这些都是优质的衬衣）. They are all made of real silk. ⑦_____（我建议你挑紫色的）. It's the fashionable color this year.

T：I also like it very much. Is it colorfast?

G: Yes, it is, and it is washable. But I would suggest that you ⑧ _____ _____ (温水洗,不要揉搓).

T: Right then. I would like to buy it.

3. Listen and fill in the blanks.

Mr. Baker asks Wang Hui whether there's anything he could do to __①__. Although his parents are __②__ after the tour, he is still __③__. Then Wang Hui advises him to have a __④__. There's bath and __⑤__ in the hotel. Besides, they provide __⑥__ and drinks for the tourists to choose from.

4. Simulation.

Suppose you are a shop assistant at a local specialties store, the tourists wants to buy some handicrafts. Make a short dialogue with your partner.

Task 2　Arts and Crafts

◇Lead-in

Some of the tourists wants to buy some arts and crafts and ask Simon to give them some advice. Simon recommends porcelain and takes the guests to the shop.

◇Analyzing the Task

Simon should do as the following.

① To have a good knowledge of arts and crafts.

② To know how to introduce arts and crafts.

The on-the-spot communication is as following.

(A＝the shop assistant　　B＝Mrs. Bell　　C＝Simon, the local guide)

B: Hi, Simon, I'd like to buy some arts and crafts. What is worth buying?

C: What about porcelain? China is the first nation to manufacture true porcelain in the world, as suggested by its name, china.

B: I've heard of Jingdezhen. Is there any products I can buy in Hunan Province?

A: There are three porcelain capitals in China, and one is Liling City of Hunan. Liling has a 2,000-year-long history of ceramic production, and is the hometown of underglaze five-colored porcelain which is a miracle of ceramic art in Chinese ceramics. Underglaze five-colored porcelains produced in Liling were exhibited at many business fairs and won gold medals in many trade events. Liling porcelains are seen as the equal of Jingdezhen porcelains.

B: Sounds great! I'd like to go and see. Would you please take me to some shops?

C: My pleasure.

(After they arrived at a porcelain shop)

B: It is extremely beautiful. This is the very thing I've been dreaming of.

A: You've made a good choice. This tea set is unusual. It was made in Liling, Hunan Province.

B: What's the feature of Liling porcelain?

A: Liling porcelain is "White as jade, clear as glass, thin as paper, ringing as a bell".

B: Oh, it must be most precious. Can I have a look?

A: Yes, sir.

B: No wonder it's so expensive. I'll take it.

A: Shall I wrap them together or separately?

B: Separately, please. What do they come to in round figures?

A: Altogether 356 yuan.

B: Here is 360 yuan.

A: (Counting money) Sir, there are thirty notes of ten yuan and six notes of five yuan, so it is 330 yuan in all. Would you please check it, sir?

B: I'm awfully sorry. I've made a mistake. I took five for ten. Here's another thirty yuan.

◇ **Developing Tasks**

1. Listen and fill in the blanks.

Shop Assistant: Good afternoon, sir. May I help you?

Mr. Brown: Yes. I'd like to buy some special local ① _____ for my family.

Shop Assistant: OK. How about some porcelain?

Mr. Brown: Well, that's rather ② _____.

Shop Assistant: Don't worry. We'll have it wrapped.

Mr. Brown: Thanks, but I have a long way to get home. Besides, they look too ③_____.

Shop Assistant: I see. How about some wooden products, then? There are many wooden products in our shop.

Mr. Brown: That would be fine.

Shop Assistant: All the wooden are in this section: wood sculptures, wooden chopsticks, and so on.

Mr. Brown: These ④_____ look nice! How much are they?

Shop Assistant: 300 yuan. Ladies usually like them.

Mr. Brown: I agree. I'll take these two.

Shop Assistant: OK. I'll wrap them up for you. Would you like anything else. For example some ⑤_____ or local delicacies?

Mr. Brown: Could you ⑥_____ some gifts for children or the elderly?

Shop Assistant: Sure. These jade talismans and bracelets are quite nice. They make good gifts for children or the elderly.

Mr. Brown: Good. I'll take some.

2. Translate the following sentences into Chinese.

① You should dial the international access code 011 plus your country code 86, and the cell phone number you want to call. But if it is a telephone, you should plus your city code before the phone number. Thus you can make an oversea call to China.

② If you want to phone someone in the city, you can call directly from your room. You need to press 0 first and when you hear the tone, press the number you want. If you want, you can also make a collect call.

3. Translate the following sentences into English.

① 福建的脱胎漆器与北京的景泰蓝、景德镇的瓷器并称为中国三大传统手工艺品。

② 中国画以其悠久的历史、独特的风格、鲜明的民族特色在世界上享有很高的声誉。

③ 我国刺绣绣工精细,图案漂亮。

④ 中国的手工艺品门类繁多,品种丰富。

⑤ 檀香扇不仅是艺术欣赏品,也是一种具有实用价值的日用品。

4. Simulation.

Three students are to play the role of a local guide, a tourist, and a shopping assistant. They meet in a tea store and the tourist wants to buy some green tea. They make a deal after bargaining.

Task 3   Tea

◇Lead-in

Some of the tourists want to buy Chinese tea to take home. They ask Simon to give them a brief introduction of Chinese tea and recommend them some famous Chinese tea to take home.

◇Analyzing the Task

Simon should know exactly the main varieties of Chinese tea and also he should tell the tourists how to choose Chinese tea and the function of the tea they want to buy.

The on-the-spot communication is as following.

(G=the tour guide   T=the tourist   S=the shop assistant)

T: Hi, Simon, Chinese tea is famous. Can you give us more details?

G: Tea is an important part of Chinese tradition. Tea has an extremely close relationship to Chinese culture, and its study covers a wide field and has very rich content. The history of Chinese tea is a long and gradual story of refinement. The original idea is credited to the legendary Emperor Shennong, who is said to have lived 5,000 years ago. A story goes that, one summer day, while visiting a distant part of his realm, he and the court stopped to rest. The servants began to boil water for the court to drink. Dried leaves from a nearby bush fell into the boiling water, and a brown substance was infused into the water. As a scientist, the Emperor was interested in the new liquid, drank some, and found it very refreshing. And so, according to legend, tea was created in 2737 B. C.

The main varieties of Chinese tea are classified as green tea, black tea, Oolong tea, white tea, yellow tea, and dark tea. Green tea is the oldest category of Chinese tea.

It is Chinese traditional custom that a host has to serve a visiting guest a cup of tea firstly when he enters his house.

T: Are there any famous tea in Hunan Province?

G: In our Hunan, we have some famous tea, for example, Anhua dark tea, Dongtinghu biluochun, Junshanyinzhen and so on.

T: Any differences?

G: Dongtinghu biluochun is a kind of green tea. Junshanyinzhen is a kind of yellow tea. China is the only producing place of yellow tea in the world. Compared with green tea, the process for making yellow tea is time-consuming and difficult.

T: What about Anhua dark tea?

G: The dark tea's main functionality ingredient is a multi-carbohydrate compound. This kind of compound may adjust in vivo sugar metabolism (prevent diabetes), reduce blood fat and blood pressure, as well as sharpen organism immunity ability. OK, now, we are here at the tea shop. You can get off the bus and have a look at the tea you'd like to buy.

T: Thanks, Simon, thank you for your introduction of Chinese tea.

(The tourists walk into the tea shop)

S: Good morning, what can I do for you?

T: We'd like to buy some Chinese tea to take home.

S: We have all kinds of Chinese tea.

T: We want to have a look by ourselves, and we'll tell you if we need you.

S: OK. It's my pleasure.

◇ **Developing Tasks**

1. Complete the following dialogue in English with the information given.

(A = the local guide   B = the tour leader   C = the tour member)

A: ① _____? （顺便问一下，你们要不要买些皮包回去？）This town is very well-known for its leather products.

C: My goodness! You can never see a guide not trying to get you into some store!

A: Relax, sir. ② _____.（我只是提供一个购物的机会，完全不是一定要你们买什么东西）

B: Never mind, dear. He doesn't mean to hurt you. I'm sure quite a few members are interested.

A: Good. ③ _____.（这家店还提供冰茶水。是免费的）

B: Wonderful. I'm thirsty now and would like to have a try. How much time do we have?

  A: ④ _____ ? (我想大约四十分钟吧。您认为够吗?)

  B: OK. I'll try to push them. By the way, do salespersons here speak English?

  A: ⑤ _____ . (当然会说。至少足够做好他们的工作了)

2. Simulation.

Three students are to play the roles of a local guide, a tourist, and a shopping assistant. They are at a store which sells silk products. The tourist is trying to buy something for his wife. The local guide and the shopping assistant help him to make a choice.

3. Put the following Chinese into English.

① 要记住,通常大多数游客的兴趣在于观光而非购物,所以要避免频繁安排购物,以免顾客厌倦和反感。

② 为了提高市场竞争力,旅行社通常付给导游很低的报酬,这使得工资之外的小费和佣金几乎成了导游获取相对较好收入的唯一途径。

4. Listen and fill in the blanks.

During the Spring Festival holidays, visiting a __①__ is one of the most important activities. The history of temple fairs may be __②__ back to the Yuan dynasty, when they were closely __③__ with Buddhist or Taoist __④__ . The fairs held at the ancient temples, and later became centers of __⑤__ worship, entertainment and __⑥__ .

A temple fair is a type of __⑦__ in China. There are performances such as __⑧__ and martial arts, numerous kinds of local snacks and other items. In recent years, the temple fair has become a place for people to __⑨__ traditional arts and experience traditional __⑩__ .

In recent years, there have been over 10 major temple fairs held each year in Beijing. Chinese people still love going to temple fairs held each year in Beijing. Chinese people still love going to temple fairs during the Spring Festival holidays. Organizers are also making __⑪__ to the events to __⑫__ the times.

◇ Related Knowledge

1. Related special terms.

(1) Where to buy.

shopping center 购物中心   shopping mall 商业街

district 区   residential area 居民区,住宅区

urban 市区的

outskirts 郊区

bazaar 市场

flea market 跳蚤市场

art museum 美术馆

suburb 近郊区

department store 百货公司

market 市场,集市

junk shop 旧货店

art gallery 画廊

(2) Handicrafts.

paper craft 纸工艺品

lacquer ware 漆器

sculpture 雕塑

charcoal carving 炭雕

wooden crafts 木制工艺品

home decoration 家居装饰

Chinese painting 国画

feather fan 羽毛扇

candle craft 蜡制工艺品

bronze ware 青铜器

clay carving 泥塑

wood carving 木刻

puppet 玩偶

tablecloth 台布

vase 花瓶

2. Useful sentences.

(1) Offering help.

◇ What can I do for you?

◇ Anything I can do for you, Madam?

◇ You can change money there.

◇ The prices there are very good.

◇ They have all the things you need.

(2) Getting information.

◇ What time do you open/close?

◇ Can you cut him a deal?

◇ Can she pay by credit card?

◇ Can you wrap this for her?

◇ Do you have any other colors?

◇ How much is it?

◇ How much does it cost?

(3) Making comments.

◇ You look great in this shirt!

◇ This color suits you well.

◇ This hat and your shoes are a perfect match.

◇ This blouse doesn't match your boots.

(4) Bargaining.

◇ What's your general price range?

◇ What price do you have in mind?

◇ The price is reasonable, taking into consideration the superior quality.

◇ That's a bit more than what you are supposed to pay.

◇ The prices have already been reduced greatly.

◇ You'd better offer no more than $40.

◇ How about splitting the difference?

◇ You have to strike a balance, if you wish to get somewhere.

◇ That's almost cost price.

◇ That's a rock-bottom price.

◇ That's the best we can get.

◇ They'll bring the price down to $50 a piece, if you are going to make a big purchase.

◇ It's a little overpriced.

◇ I like everything about it except the price.

◇ I've seen this cheaper in other places.

◇ Can you make it cheaper?

◇ Can it (they) be cheaper?

◇ Can you come down a little?

(5) Making payment.

◇ Cash or charge?

◇ Would you like to pay cash or charge?

◇ Will you pay by cash or credit card?

◇ Cash, please.

◇ Can I use VISA?

◇ Do you accept/take VISA?

◇ Can I pay by installment payment?

◇ Can I pay in Japanese yen?

◇ Do you take / accept Japanese yen?

(6) Others.

◇ Please wrap it.

◇ I'd like to return this.

◇ Do you have a receipt?

◇ Could you exchange this, please?

◇ It's got a stain. / It has a stain.

◇ Can I have a refund?

◇ I'd like to get a refund, please. / I'd like a refund, please.

◇ I'd like my money back, please.

Module 12
Recreational Program

Recreational programs are essential to a pleasing, interesting and satisfying trip. Various recreational activities provided in theaters, sports venues, pubs and bars, and other venues all give tourists good choices to relax or experience the local life while spending their holidays.

On the one hand, people are paying more attention to their health. Even during their travel, they would like to maintain their health and fitness routines, either go to a gym or a swimming pool which is easily accessible in a hotel. Hot springs or golf courses may be available at some resort hotels. On the other hand, overseas visitors want to explore the local culture or do as the locals do. Big cities and popular tourist destinations are always abundant in multiple entertainment activities and colorful nightlife. Watching folk performances, going to pubs, singing halls and dance halls and so on are all available in Changsha.

The tour guide should arrange proper entertainments accordingly. What's more, the tour guide should make efforts to get himself familiar with all relevant information, knowledge and understanding of the recreational activities, so that he can introduce them effectively to the tourists.

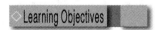

Knowledge

① Familiar with the recreational programs of the tourist destination.

② Master the vocabulary and expressions related to recreational activities.

Skills

① Be able to introduce recreational facilities and services.

② Be able to introduce Chinese folk art to tourists.

③ Be able to introduce Chinese culture and customs to tourists.

Quality

① Enhance ability in serving tourists.

② Enrich culture awareness related to local and domestic traditions.

Task 1　Health Activities

◇Lead-in

After diner, Simon and all his group members are staying at Sheraton Changsha Hotel to have a rest. A tourist is approaching to him and asking him about the fitness facilities and services provided in the hotel. As a tour guide, how should Simon respond to the tourist's inquiries?

◇Analyzing the Task

As a tour guide, Simon should do as follows.

① Get familiar with the hotel fitness facilities and services.

As a tour guide, you should make a full preparation so that you can provide your tourists with the best service. If this is your first time to stay in this hotel, you can get the information about the hotel facilities and services through its official website. Or you can ask the hotel front desk clerks about it. If this is not your first time to stay in the same hotel, you should keep in mind the basic knowledge about the hotel service, including fitness service.

② Introduce hotel fitness service in a clear and proper manner.

The on-the-spot communication is as following.

(T=the tourist　　G=the tour guide)

(A tourist is asking the local guide Simon about the fitness center)

T: Simon, we don't have any arrangement for tonight, right?

G: Yes, Mike. How was your day?

T: A very pleasant day. Thank you, Simon. The scenic spot we visited today is fascinating.

G: I'm so glad that you enjoyed it. What impressed you most?

T: Well, the culture relics we saw today helped me understand Chinese culture better.

G: That's good. Do you have any plan for tonight?

T: Well, I wonder if there is a fitness center in the hotel?

G: Sure, there is. The fitness center is on the 6th floor.

T: What facilities do they have?

G: The hotel provides outstanding fitness facilities, including a gymnasium, a sauna, a table tennis room, an aerobics room and an indoor swimming pool.

T: Excellent. I want to swim later this evening. Is is too late?

G: Don't worry. It opens for 24 hours.

T: Do they charge a fee?

G: No, they are complimentary to hotel guests. , but don't forget to bring your key card.

T: Thank you, Simon. You are so helpful.

G: It's my pleasure. Have fun.

◇ Developing Tasks

1. Translate the following sentences into English.

① 酒店提供全方位的休闲娱乐设施及服务。

② 健身中心提供宽敞的运动空间及最新款式的时尚健身器材。

③ 健身中心对酒店客人免费开放。

④ 恒温室内游泳池位于酒店6楼。

⑤ 7楼的桑拿中心是缓解疲劳、放松身心的好去处。

2. Listen to the recording and fill in the blanks of the passage.

Chinese Kung Fu

The origins of Chinese Kung Fu can be found over 6,000 years ago, when men were taught to hunt and fight. Nowadays, it is regarded as a ① gaining more and more popularity and even stands as a ② for Chinese culture. Styles including Shaolin, Tai Chi and Qigong have many followers ③ . Some Westerners think that all Chinese people are ④ . That's not true, but this traditional heritage has its ⑤ in modern times and left much ⑥ on the locals' ⑦ .

Although being fighting styles, Kung Fu advocates virtue and peace, not aggression or violence. This has been the common value upheld by martial artists ⑧ . With a number of movement sets, boxing styles, weapon skills and some fighting stunts, Kung Fu keeps its original function of ⑨ . Now its value in body-building and ⑩ is also highly appreciated.

3. Simulation.

Student A: You are a tourist who wants to do some workout while staying in the hotel, so you go to ask your local guide about the fitness facilities and service available in the hotel.

Student B: You are a local guide. A tourist is asking you about the hotel facilities and service. Introduce the hotel facilities and service in a polite and patient way.

Task 2　Watch Shows

◇Lead-in

There is no arrangement tonight, so some tourists want to watch a show to kill time. They are curious about the show. One of them is asking Simon, the tour guide, what the show is about. As a tour guide, you are responsible for answering tourists' questions related to performances as well as introducing the local culture to overseas visitors.

◇Analyzing the Task

As a tour guide you should do as follows.

① Familiar with local folk art.

Recreational activities are absolutely necessary for a pleasant tour. It is entertainment as well as a way to experience the local culture. A tour guide should hence make efforts to get himself familiar with the traditional art forms.

② Offer guiding service in a courteous and clear manner.

The on-the-spot communication is as following.

(T=the tourist   G=the tour guide)

(A tour guide is discussing an acrobatic show with his tourists)

T: Simon. We are quite interested in the show. We knew it from the brochure. It says it is a must to do in the city.

G: Yes. Mr. Vincent. If you want to watch it, I can book tickets for you.

T: T: Would you tell us more about the performance?

G: Sure. The performance is one of the best in the city. It is a blend of traditional elements with modern trends, containing cross talks, skits, folk art forms, acrobatics, singing and dancing.

T: Chinese acrobatics are impressive.

G: Yes. It is something you can't miss while traveling in China. Its Chinese name is zaji. Za means variety; ji means art and skills. Acrobatics are the performance of extraordinary feats of balance, agility and motor coordination.

T: I've seen it on TV in England. An acrobat holding sticks with spinning plates on top in both hands makes a swift back flip from a table to the ground.

G: Modern acrobatics mainly depend on the performer's soft body to complete a series of highly difficult movement.

T: I hope I will see for myself today, for I've never had a chance to see a live acrobatic show.

G: Plate spinning is a classic program. What you are going to see today is a mixture of acrobatics, contemporary dance and modern technology.

T: I bet it must be a fascinating performance. I can't wait. What time should we go to the theater?

G: The show starts at 9:15 p.m., so we are leaving at 8:00 p.m. Now, I'll book tickets for you first.

◇Developing Tasks

1. Translate the following sentences into English.

① 在中国,多样的娱乐活动如歌舞、歌剧、相声、电影等,能让你大饱眼福和耳福。

② 我们今晚去剧院看变脸表演。

③ 请大家晚上 7:30 在酒店大堂集合。

④ 来中国旅游却不去欣赏京剧,那是个极大的遗憾。

⑤ 杂技表演是中国人最喜爱的艺术形式之一。

2. Listen to the recording and fill in the blanks of the passage.

<h3 style="text-align:center">Hunan Flower Drum Opera</h3>

Hunan Huaguxi, literally known as Hunan Flower Drum Opera, is a form of ___①___ originating in Hunan Province. It is known in China for its ___②___, and is often referred to as the "spicy" form of Chinese opera. Huaguxi is known to have existed ___③___ 1695, during the ___④___. Unlike other forms of Chinese opera, Huaguxi originally had only ___⑤___. These including xiaochou, a small male clown, and xiaodan, a vivacious young girl. The ___⑥___ was played by men until women entered Chinese opera in the early 20th century. In the mid-18th century, a xiaosheng role was added. This role refers to handsome young males.

Most Huaguxi plays were originally xiaoxi, ___⑦___ lasting an hour or less. These plays often dealt with everyday rural life. With the rise of professional Huaguxi ___⑧___ and performances in the capital city of Changsha, longer plays, daxi, began to be performed. These plays dealt with grander themes of social satire and class struggle. Like other forms of Chinese opera, Huaguxi is staged with very few ___⑨___. Music accompanying Huaguxi reflects the Changsha ___⑩___ spoken in Hunan. It is played with instruments like datong (fiddle), yueqin (moon lute), dizi (bamboo flute), and suona (oboe). Percussion instruments provide the basic tempo for the performance.

3. Simulation.

Student A: You are a tourist who is curious about the Flower Drum Opera. Ask your tour guide several questions about it.

Student B: You are a local guide. A tourist is asking you about the performance you are going to see tonight. Introduce the Flower Drum Opera to your tourist, including the history, features of this opera.

Task 3   Pubs and Bars

◇Lead-in

Since there is no particular arrangement tonight. The tourists are considering what they are going to do to spend their last night in the city. Some tourists want to experience the hustle and bustle of the local life. A tourist is coming for your suggestions about the pubs and bars in the city. As a tour guide, please give your tourists some recommendations and introduce the nightlife culture of the city.

◇ Analyzing the Task

As a tour guide, Simon should do as following.

① Get himself familiar with the local lifestyles and entertainment

As a tour guide, you should know that nightlife in Changsha city is an experience that travelers should not miss, as it represents an unforgettable and dynamic local culture. Local people usually enjoy going to bars, clubs, KTV, cafes, tea-houses, cinemas and theaters. In Changsha, pubs and bars boast a style all its own. Romantic, quiet bars, dynamic show bars, tea-houses, western style restaurants... definitely something for everyone.

② Give the guests professional advice

The on-the-spot communication is as following.

Dialogue 1: A tour guide is discussing an acrobatic show with his tourists

(T=the tourist   G=the tour guide)

G: George, there is no arrangement tonight. So, what's your plan?

T: You know, Susie and I have different opinions, so we don't have any plans yet.

G: Changsha is regarded as "a city of entertainment" in China, because it has a series of famous entertainment programs held by Hunan Television and rich and colorful nightlife. Watching folk performances, we have already done that last night, right? Pubs, cafes, singing halls and dance halls and so on are also available in Changsha.

T: Well, I heard the city has a lot of bars and pubs.

G: That's a good choice. You and Susie can go for a couple of drinks. Bars are good places to know the city and its people, besides they are ideal places to relax.

T: Yeah. I read it in the brochure that going to a bar is a must to do here in this city.

G: Uh huh. There are many featured bars in the city, where local snacks and refreshing beverages are served alongside a live DJ.

T: You know, we have a lot of bars and pubs in England as well. People love to have a cup of drink with friends after work.

G: I've heard that before. You know, local people here also like to spend their nights at pubs and bars. Most bars and pubs are located in downtown area which are not far away from our hotel. Hope you guys have a wonderful night.

T: Thank you. See you.

G: See you.

Dialogue 2: Ordering drinks and snacks in a bar

(T=the tourist   G=the tour guide   W=the waitress)

W: Good evening, ladies and gentlemen. How many people are there in your party?

G: Three.

W: This way please. How about this table?

G: OK. Thanks.

W: Here is the wine list and the snack list is on the other side. You guys want to have a look first?

G: Sure.

W: Please let me know when you are ready to order.

G: Let's see... cocktail, brandy, Scotch, rum, wines... local beer. What do you guys want to drink?

T: I want to try local beer.

G: Good, then we'll have 3 bottles of beer. How about snacks?

T: Let's me see. I'd like to have the grilled squids. It looks delicious.

G: OK, grilled squids, and one fruit plate.

W: Sir, you ordered 3 bottles of local beer, grilled squids, and one fruit plate. Is that right?

G: Yes.

W: I'll be right back with your order in a minute.

◇ Developing Tasks

1. Translate the following sentences into English.

① 酒吧在英国人的生活中所扮演的角色和美国的咖啡馆、中国的茶馆一样,都是当地文化中不可缺少的一部分。

② 英国的酒吧从字面意义上来说分为 pub、bar 和 club,pub 是最大众化的,也是英国历史最悠久的酒吧类型。

③ 英国的酒吧文化有着一千多年的悠久历史。

④ 英国的酒吧文化传统与美国的不同。

⑤ 最受英国人欢迎的啤酒是常温的黑啤。

2. Listen to the recording and fill in the blanks of the passage.

What is a Pub?

The word pub is ___①___ public house. There are over 60,000 pubs in the UK. Pubs are an important part of British life. People talk, eat, drink, meet their friends and ___②___ there. Pubs often have two bars, one usually ___③___ than the other, many have a ___④___ where people can sit in the summer. Children can go in pub gardens with their ___⑤___.

Groups of friends normally buy "rounds" of drinks, where the person whose turn it is will buy drinks for all the members of the group. It is sometimes difficult to get served when pubs are busy: people do not ___⑥___, but the bar ___⑦___ will usually try and serve those who have been waiting the longest at the bar first. If you spill a stranger's drink ___⑧___, it is good manners and prudent to offer to buy another drink. Most pubs offer a complete range of beers, local and imported, with German, Belgian and French beers being in demand.

Although most people think pubs are places where people drink alcohol, pubs in fact sell ___⑨___, too. British people drink an average of 99.4 ___⑩___ of beer every year. More than 80% of this beer is drunk in pubs and clubs.

3. Simulation.

Student A: You are a tourist from England. You want to go to a local bar or pub tonight with your friends. Now you are asking your tour guide for the recommendations of the local pubs and bars.

Student B: You are a local guide. A tourist is asking for your advice about the local pubs and bars. Introduce the local pubs and bars to your tourist.

Task 4 Traditional Chinese Entertainment

◇Lead-in

Traditional Chinese entertainment is an import element that attracts tourists from overseas.

Frank is a young man from England who loves Chinese culture a lot. He'd seen the lion dance in China town in London for several times. Now he is discussing the traditional Chinese entertainment with the tour guide Simon.

◇ **Analyzing the Task**

As a tour guide, Simon should do as follows.

① Get himself familiar with traditional Chinese entertainment

Besides providing guide service to your tourists, as a local guide, you should work as a spreader of Chinese culture or at least local culture so that more overseas visitors have a better understanding of China when they are back to their own countries. To do so, you should get yourself familiar with local traditional customs and culture. In some scenic spots, there are always some traditional Chinese entertainment programs or performances arranged. As a tour guide, you should bear in mind what programs you are going to watch, and introduce the origins, meaning, customs, etc. to your visitors.

② Provide tour guide service

The on-the-spot communication is as following.

(T=the tourist   G=the tour guide)

(A tour guide is discussing the lion dance with a tourist when they are watching it)

T: Simon, is this the lion dance?

G: Yes. Have you ever heard of it?

T: I've seen it before when I was in London. You know, there are lion dance performances in China town every year during the Chinese New Year.

G: Do you know why lion dances take place during the first few days of the Chinese New Year?

T: I've never thought about it. I think it will bring good luck in a new year to come.

G: You are right. According to traditional Chinese belief, the lion signifies courage, stability and superiority. The lion dance is performed to chase away ghosts and evil spirits, and since the monsters, ghosts, evil spirits and giants like nian are afraid of loud noises, the dance has become a natural complement to the fire crackers' noise.

T: I see. It must have a long history then.

G: Lion dances may have been recorded in China as early as the third century AD. There are various styles of lions and lion dances, though the biggest distinction is the Northern and the Southern. I believe what you've seen in London is the Southern lion dance.

T: What's the Northern lion dance?

G: The Northern lion dance was used for entertaining the Imperial Court. The lions show more of a lion's flowing mane. The appearance is similar of a fu lion, a Pekinese.

T: That's very interesting. How about the Southern lion dance?

G: The Southern lions are divided into two main groups and performed during Chinese New Year celebrations. The appearance of the lion and the color of the fur have symbolism as well.

T: So, what does this black lion symbolize?

G: The black lion is considered the youngest lion, and the movement of this lion should be fast like a young child or a headstrong teenager.

T: Look! The Lion is blinking his eyes at me. It is a naughty lion, isn't it?

◇ Developing Tasks

1. Translate the following sentences into English.

① 中国的舞狮有时会和舞龙混淆。

② 每头狮子由两个人合作表演，一人舞头，一人舞尾。

③ 这个舞狮表演真是栩栩如生。

④ 舞狮是为了来年给人们带来好运和幸福。

⑤ 舞狮有南北之分。

2. Listen to the recording and fill in the blanks of the passage.

Dragon Dances

Dragons are of course legendary animals, but they are important to Chinese people who think of dragons as helpful, friendly creatures. They are linked to good luck, long life and ___①___ . They are nothing like the fierce, fire-breathing Western dragons that carry off princesses and eat people. Chinese dragons are ___②___ storm clouds and life-giving rain. They have special power so they can fly in the air, swim in the sea and walk on land. The dragon has features of other animals such as the ___③___ of a stag, the ___④___ of a fish and the footpads of a tiger.

Dragon dances are ___⑤___ at New Year to scare away evil spirits. During the dance the performers hold poles and raise and lower the dragon. Sometimes one man has a "Pearl of Wisdom" on a pole and he entices the dragon to follow him to the beat of a ___⑥___ , as if searching for wisdom and ___⑦___ .

Dragons used in dragon dances vary in ___⑧___ from a few meters to up to 100 m long. Longer dragons are thought to be more ___⑨___ than shorter ones. The dances can be performed either during the day or night, but at night a blazing ___⑩___ will be carried to light the way.

3. Simulation.

Student A: You are a tourist from England. You are interested in traditional Chinese entertainment. You are asking your local guide about the dragon dance.

Student B: You are a local guide. A tourist is asking you about the dragon dance. Introduce it to your tourist. It's origin, meaning, forms, performers, etc.

1. Dragon boat races.

The dragon boat race is one of the most typical traditions of Chinese Dragon Boat Festival which falls on the fifth day of the fifth lunar month. The activity is widely held in southern and northeastern areas of China where rivers and lakes are densely scattered. With a far-reaching history of more than 2,000 years, the observance can be dated back to the boat racing to save the ancient Chinese poet Qu Yuan in the Warring States Period. Now it becomes a worldwide popular water sport and celebrating activity spreading to Southeast Asian countries like Vietnam, Singapore, and Malaysia.

What is a dragon boat like?

In a long and narrow shape, a traditional dragon boat is a kind of watercraft made of teak wood, with paddles on both sides. About 20-30 yards long and 1-2 yards wide, the fore and aft of the boat are decorated with a dragon's turnup head and tail. The body of the boat is carved or painted with traditional auspicious patterns like waves, clouds or beasts in bright colors such as red, blue, green, black and gold. Apart from decorative items, there are also pennants and drums, which are used for guiding the paddlers' movement. In different regions, the boat's designs and sizes are varied slightly. Now the dragon boat race has become a worldwide water competition, and big changes take place in the boats' shape, materials as well as decoration regalia.

Origin and history

With a history over 2,000 years, dragon boat races had gone through three stages, including ceremonial, commemorative and competitive functions. The dragon is an imaginary creature which has advantages of all other animals. Ancient Chinese people regarded themselves as the descendents of the dragon, and they took the dragon as their totem. Therefore, people made boats in a dragon image and held racing games. It was usually for totem worshipping or other jubilant occasions, such as sowing and harvesting seasons.

About in 278 BC, the great patriotic statesman of Chu Kingdom, Qu Yuan, witnessed his homeland was shattered, and he committed suicide by drowning himself with stones in a river. People raced out boats to retrieve his body, and then the performance became a defined custom of the Dragon Boat Festival. Around in 1970s, the race turned to be a competitive water sport, which is enjoyed worldwide and brought to international sport events.

Crew of the boat

The crew of a dragon boat usually consists of a drummer, a sweep and paddlers. The number of the paddlers varies accordingly since the boats are in different sizes. The main force comes from the paddlers who actuate the boat, and the drummer is in charge of guiding the frequency and synchronicity of all the paddlers' movement. Meanwhile, the drumbeat is also a useful way to inspire the crew's spirits in the competition. The sweep plays a very critical role, for he/she takes control of the moving direction of the boat and guarantees the safety of the other members, and mostly the role is undertaken by professional coaches.

Pre-ceremony before the race

Before the race, there are ceremonies to welcome the dragon boat, worship the gods or commemorate the great figures like Qu Yuan. In some places, people will kill a rooster and drop its blood on the dragon's head, or a pair of paper roosters is placed on the boat, which is believed able to protect the crew's safety.

Dragon boat race schedule and destinations in Hunan

The Miluo River in Yueyang is the very one that Qu Yuan drown himself to death, which is also the birthplace of dragon boat culture. There will be standard competitions held in Miluo River Dragon Boat Race Center on the festival day. All the athletes are professional players, and visitors can surely watch a fierce and thrilling competition.

In Phoenix Ancient Town, the boat race is an old tradition. The race retains the original rules and mode, and after the competition, there is usually a game of catching ducks for rewarding the crew, which is also full of fun.

2. Changsha nightlife.

The peak time for night life in the city is during the period from one to two o'clock. This is when the streets are jammed with cars, enthusiastic crowds and shrewd peddlers. Around twelve, it is very hard to find an available taxi near the main thoroughfares.

Some people think that to enjoy the nightlife of Changsha, you may have four steps: the first is foot massage, the second is passing time in pubs, the third is singing in the KTV, and the last one is trying midnight snacks. In the downtown of Changsha, there are many footbath centers. Put feet in the wooden basin with warm milk or in the warm water with Chinese herbal medicines or flowers, then the massage man cleans your feet and gives a massage to your legs, feet, arms and head. It will take about one hour to finish the footbath.

After that, you can go to pubs or bars. If you were accompanied by friends, it would be more pleasant. Then, if you'd love to, you may sing several songs in the KTV. Now, most Chinese KTVs provide not only Chinese songs but also English, Japanese, Korean and French songs. When you leave the KTV for your accommodation, you can have some midnight snacks if you feel a little hungry.

3. Watching lanterns and guessing lantern riddles.

During the Han dynasty, Buddhism flourished in China. So in order to popularize Buddhism, one of the emperors gave an order to light lanterns in the imperial palace to worship and show respect for Buddha on the 15th day of the first lunar month. During the Tang, Song, Ming and Qing dynasties, lighting lanterns became a tradition for Chinese people.

Today, when festivals come, red lanterns can be seen in the street, in each house, and stores. In parks, lanterns of various shapes and types attract countless visitors.

Beginning from the Song dynasty, guessing riddles is regarded as an indispensable part of the Lantern Festival. People write all kinds of riddles on pieces of paper, and paste them on colorful lanterns to let visitors guess. Gifts are presented to the people who get the right answers. Because this intellectual activity is exciting, people from all walks of life enjoy it.

4. Walking on stilts.

Walking on stilts, another folk art, traces its origins to the Spring and Autumn period. Performers not only walk on stilts by binding them to their feet, but also do some breathtaking moves. As actors impersonate different characters like monks, clowns, and fishermen and perform vivid and humorous acts, the art amuses many people.

5. Useful sentences.

(1) Health activities.

◇ The gymnasium is very modern.

◇ The hotel has a wide range of entertainment and fitness facilities to your delight.

◇ Our fitness center is located on the 7th floor.

◇ The fitness center opens from 6 a.m. to 12 midnight including Sunday.

◇ It is a heated swimming pool.

◇ If you feel tired, you can enjoy a professional foot massage here to make your travel more comfortable.

◇ A wide range of workout programs are provided in the hotel.

◇ Doing aerobics for an hour is greatly different from lifting weights.

◇ Some of the services and facilities listed may not be available on a 24-hour basis or without advance requests.

◇ The fitness center is open to the hotel guests for free.

◇ Fees on certain facilities and services may apply.

◇ You can also play table tennis here.

◇ Kung Fu is also one of the most precious parts of Chinese culture.

◇ Taiji is an internal Chinese martial art practiced for both its defense training and its health benefits.

(2) Watch a show.

◇ We are going to watch a local opera tonight.

◇ The play starts at 8 p.m.

◇ We need to get tickets at the box office.

◇ We are in Row 6, Seat 2 and Seat 4.

◇ There's still some time before the performance begins.

◇ Here is the program.

◇ I was really touched by the play.

◇ It is quite different from operas in the West.

◇ Chinese opera is a popular form of drama and musical theatre in China with roots going back as far as the third century.

◇ There are numerous regional branches of Chinese opera.

◇ Beijing opera is one of the most notable operas in China.

◇ The operas draw their themes from Chinese historical events, fictional tales, and classical literary works.

◇ Acrobatics are performances of extraordinary feats of balance, agility, and motor coordination.

◇ Both of the acrobats should balance themselves perfectly, and coordinate his movement with the other.

◇ What do you think of the show?

(3) Pubs and bars.

◇ Our city has always been a very hospitable place and that is reflected in the quality and range of its many pubs and bars.

◇ The word pub is short for public house.

◇ Most pubs offer a complete range of beer, local and imported.

◇ Pubs are important for people. They talk, eat, drink, meet their friends and relax there.

◇ Most pubs sell many different kinds of beer, some on tap and some in bottles.

◇ British beer is brewed from malt and hops.

◇ You can learn a lot about a culture by kicking back in a pub or bar.

◇ Some bars provide live music and entertainment.

◇ Some bars offer food in addition to drinks.

◇ This is a classical style bar, designed in a simple but classy way.

◇ This is perhaps the most famous club in the city.

◇ This bar blurs the line between a Western-style bar and a Chinese-style bar.

◇ What would you like to drink?

◇ Do you know any local beer?

◇ Could you recommend some good and inexpensive alcohol?

(4) Traditional Chinese entertainment.

◇ The lion dance is a form of traditional dance in Chinese culture and other Asian countries.

◇ There are various styles of lions and lion dances.

◇ Performers will mimic a lion's movements in a lion costume.

◇ The lion dance is usually performed during the Chinese New Year and other Chinese traditional, cultural and religious events.

◇ The lion dance is normally operated by two dancers.

◇ Chinese lion dance fundamental movements can be found in most Chinese martial arts.

◇ There are two main forms of the Chinese lion dance, the Northern Lion and the Souther Lion.

◇ The Chinese Southern Lion originated from Guangdong.

◇ The dragon dance is performed by a team of dancers.

◇ Chinese dragons are believed to bring good luck to people.

◇ The longer the dragon in the dance, the more luck it will bring to the community.

◇ Lantern riddles are riddles written on the lanterns and displayed during the Chinese lantern festival or middle-autumn day. The full name of lantern riddles are riddles written on lanterns.

◇ Traditional Chinese entertainments are passed down from generation to generation with most of which are kept to its origins.

◇ In the lantern festival, people will carry lanterns and go to the streets at night to watch lion or dragon dances, guess lantern riddles and light fireworks.

◇ Most of traditional entertainments are kept as festival traditions.

Module 13
Seeing off Guests

    Seeing off tourists is the last direct contact between the guide and the tourists, which is also vital throughout the whole reception process in tourism. A happy ending will give a good impression to the tourists. In the end of the seeing off service, the tour guide also must show his hospitality and consideration to the tourists, as well as make use of the last time to communicate with the tourists, because he should express his thanks to the tourists and welcome them to come next time.

Learning Objectives

Knowledge

① Know the working process about seeing off guests at the airport.

② Master the vocabulary and expressions about seeing off guests.

Skills

① Be able to know how to deliver a farewell speech.

② Be able to master tips of writing a farewell speech.

③ Be able to list the layout of seeing off guests at the airport.

④ Be able to help guests get on the tour bus.

Quality

① Strengthen service consciousness and confidence.

② Foster problem-solving ability and interpersonal communication ability.

Task 1 Checking Out

◇Lead-in

Simon, a local guide from CITS, is waiting for the tour group CITS20161008A from England to check out. There are 20 members, and the tour leader is John Smith. The tourists are checking out and they will leave. What should Simon do at this moment?

◇Analyzing the Task

Simon must do as following:

① Remind the tour leader of the time to group together.

② Wait for the whole group in the hotel.

③ Check the number of the group.

④ Help the tourists check everything (personal documents, luggage, packages and so on).

⑤ Head them for the bus.

The on-the-spot communication is as following.

(S: Simon   J: John Smith   T: the tourists   D: the hotel receptionist)

S: Excuse me, all the tourists from TITICACA please come here to wait for the bus.

T: OK, we will check out first.

S: Is the tour leader here, please?

T: The leader is over there.

S: Thank you, please wait a minute. I go to meet the leader. (Simon walks to the leader) Excuse me, Mr. John Smith, can you help me check all the tour group?

J: Of course, I can.

S: And please show your tour group code.

J: Er, let me see, oh yes.

J: OK. (Everybody, follow me please)

S: Welcome to Changsha again and I hope that you had a good trip this time.

J: We're so glad you've come to see off us at the airport, Simon. And thanks to what you've done for us. You really did a great job.

S: My pleasure. Did you have a nice trip?

J: Yes, quite pleasant. But we feel a bit tired.

S: Yes. You all need a good rest. Is everyone in the group here?

J: Yes, a party of twenty-five.

S: (Simon counts the number) Yes, twenty-five. And please help me to collect the room cards, and then we can check out.

J: OK, everybody please cleans your room and takes your luggage and room card to come here.

T: Yes, we will do it as soon as possible.

S: Hello, John, how many cards do you have?

J: Twenty-five, and we have got all of them.

S: Good, let's go to the receptionist to check out.

J: Sure.

S: Excuse me, we are the tour group CITS20161008A from England. I am the tour guide. We have 25 rooms. Now, we want to check out.

D: OK. Wait for a minute. I need to check all the rooms.

S: Fine, thank you. All the tourists from CITS20161008A please wait for a moment and then we will take the bus to the airport.

T: No problem.

D: Excuse me, we checked out all the rooms and please sign your name on this paper and then you can leave.

S: That is great, thank you again.

D: Goodbye and welcome next time.

S: Thank you for all your help. I think we will choose this hotel next time. Goodbye.

S: Hello, all the tourists please come together. We will take the bus as soon as possible. So, please check your personal things and luggage again. If you need any help, please tell me.

T: OK!

S:OK, everybody. (Simon faces the group and waves his hands) Our bus is just waiting in the parking lot. Don't get lost.

J:That's fine. Hurry up, guys!

S:This way, please.

S:(Simon leads them to the bus) Here we are, ladies and gentlemen. This is our driver, Mr. Wang.

J:Nice to meet you, Mr. Wang.

S:Mr. Wang is going to help us put our luggage in the trunk.

(Then Simon stands by the bus and helps the group get on the bus. After they get on the bus, Simon counts the number to make sure everyone is on the bus. And then they head for the airport)

Developing Tasks

1. Matching.

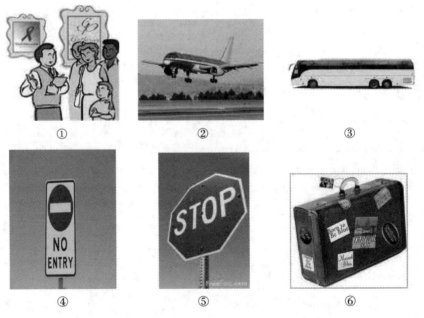

a. coach   b. tour guide   c. no entry

d. baggage   e. sign   f. flight

2. Phrases interpreting.

问询处		一行 25 人	
退房		登机牌	
托运		行李箱	
候机室		登机	
起飞时间		安检	

3. Discuss and write down.

① If you are a local guide, what preparation should be done before seeing off the guests?

_____
_____
_____
_____
_____

② What can you do to help the tourist group to check out?

_____
_____
_____
_____
_____

4. Listen and fill in the blanks.

(A＝the guide　B＝the tour leader)

A: Excuse me, ① _____?

B: Let me check it.

A: ② _____.

B: Yes, all the members are here.

A: ③ _____?

B: OK. Let us count again.

A: ④ _____.

B: Hello, everybody, let's get on the bus.

B: And great thanks to the guide. Thank you for meeting us.

A: I'm glad to be of service, Miss Smith. Welcome to Fuzhou again. ⑤ _____?

B: I'm glad to say we all love Fuzhou after this trip.

A: That's great. However, ⑥ _____.

B: Thank you again.

A: Now, ⑦ _____.

B: OK. Here you are. There are 16 pieces altogether.

A: ⑧ _____.

B: I'm glad to hear that. Shall we go now?

A: Yes, of course.

5. Simulation.

Sunny, the local guide from CITS, is seeing off Sunshine Tour Group of 26 members from Canada at Fuzhou Changle International Airport. The tour leader is James Brown. The departure time is 9 p. m. Sunny is helping the guests checking out.

Task 2　Extending a Farewell Speech

On the bus, Simon, a local guide from CITS, is delivering a farewell speech. How would Simon bid farewell to his guests? What would he say to them?

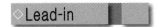

Simon can deliver a farewell speech as following.

① Express the feeling of parting.

② Deliver thanks for co-operation.

③ Make a conclusion to the trip.

④ Extend best wishes.

⑤ When presenting a farewell speech, ensure a friendly, sincere and emotional tone.

The on-the-spot communication is as following.

(S: Simon　　B: John Smith—leader of the tour group)

S: Dear guests, time flies when we are having fun. Your trip, like all good things, is coming to an end now.

B: Yes, so fast.

S: Just as a Chinese saying goes: "No feast lasts forever".

B: Yes, we think we will come again in the future.

S: So it is time to say goodbye to you although I hate to. Everytime we say goodbye, I find it hard to express myself.

B: Oh, Thank you, Simon. Thank you for coming to see us off.

S: It is really my pleasure to have been with you all the way through. In these five days, we visited a millennium academy—Yuelu Academy; we met a lady who is more than 1,000 years old in the Hunan Museum; we went to the former residence of Chairman Mao Zedong, and we enjoyed the wonderful landscape of Zhangjiajie. I believe it was an impressive experience to us all.

B: Yes, we also feel very happy during this trip and we think it is an unforgettable trip.

S: I am really glad that you have been enjoying yourselves. Your happiness really makes my day.

B: Oh, the same as us.

S: So in a word, thank you again for your cooperation, without which our tour wouldn't have been so successful. My special thanks also to John. Thank you, John. I really appreciate your help and cooperation.

B: Also thank you Simon. It's very kind of you.

S: By the way, I would like to make a sincere apology for any inconvenience if we weren't able to satisfy some of your needs despite all our efforts.

Developing Tasks

1. Discuss and write down.

① What attitude should a guide take in settling departure issues and saying farewell to his/her guests?

_____
_____
_____
_____

② Where should the tour guide deliver the farewell speech? What information should a farewell speech deliver?

_____

_____

_____

_____

2. Listen and fill in the blanks.

Ladies and Gentlemen:

Time ① quickly and your trip in Wuhan is ② to a close. It's a pity that you cannot stay in our country ③ . Then allow me to take this opportunity to say goodbye to you.

I would like to tell you that it is a ④ pleasure for me to be your guide these days. I have had the opportunity to meet and get to know you. Thank you for the ⑤ and support you gave us in the past several days. As a Chinese ⑥ saying goes, "A good friend from afar ⑦ a distant land closer." I hope you'll take happy ⑧ of your trip in China ⑨ home.

I wish to see you again in the future and to be your guide. ⑩ , thank you for your cooperation and support.

Goodbye!

3. Translation.

① Bidding farewell to guests marks the end of a tour guide's service. Wherever it is arranged to be, it is of equal importance to the welcome and should be conducted with sincerity; if anything undesirable happens at the last minute, it may ruin the entire experience of a tour. Therefore, a qualified tour guide should try to make the farewell experience impressive and everlasting.

② 如果告别环节安排得当，整个导游工作就可以成功地画上句号了，否则可能会导致游客的下一段旅程出现延误和其他问题，前功尽弃。

4. Simulation.

Three students are to play the roles of a local guide, a tourist leader, and a tourist member. Sunny, the guide from China International Travel Service, is seeing the tourists off at the airport, and giving a farewell speech. The tourists express their thankfulness.

Task 3　Departure Procedure

◇Lead-in

An England tour group have finished their trip in Changsha and Shaoshan. Simon, the local guide from CITS, is leading them to finish the leaving formalities. How can Simon do the work well?

◇Analyzing the Task

① Reach the airport ahead of time: international flights should be 2 hours, domestic flights should be 90 minutes, trains should be 1 hour in advance.

② Go through leaving formalities including delivering transportation tickets, checking the luggage, getting boarding passes, giving all the tickets, passports and boarding passes to the tour leader.

③ Bid farewell.

The on-the-spot communication is as following.

(G=the tour guide　　T=Mr. Smith)

G: Here we are at the airport. Please put your luggage on the cart. Let's go inside. (inside) Now would you please wait for me for a few minutes? I'm going to get the boarding passes and luggage checks for you.

T: OK. Take your time. And would you please also bring a few customs declaration forms?

G: Sure. (after a while) Thank you for your waiting for me. Here are your tickets, boarding passes and luggage checks. Please check them. And here are some customs declaration forms. Please fill them out if you have anything to declare.

T: Thank you.

G: My pleasure. Well, Mr. Smith, would you please pay the departure tax over there while they are filling out the forms? You have to pay that when you go through the security check, you know.

T: I see. How much is that?

G: 60 yuan per person. That's 1,260 for twenty-one.

T: OK. I'll be back right away. (after a while) It's done. Is there anything else?

G: Yes. They have got their forms ready. Shall we go for the security check now?

T: Sure. Let's go.

G: Here we are. You will be requested to show your receipt for the departure tax, your plane tickets, the group visa and your boarding passes. You'd better get them in order.

T: Yes. They are all here.

(after a while)

G: Is everything OK, Mr. Smith?

T: Yes. Thank you very much.

G: You are welcome. Well, it's really time we said goodbye to each other now. We look forward to seeing you again soon.

T: I hope so. I must say you are a very good guide. Thank you for everything you've done for us.

G: It's very kind of you to say so. Have a pleasant journey home.

T: Thank you. Goodbye

◇ Developing Tasks

1. Translation.

① group visa   ② take off

③ exit visa   ④ departure lounge

⑤ luggage rack   ⑥ mother-and-child room

⑦ 安全检查   ⑧ 超重费

⑨ 海关人员   ⑩ 免费行李

⑪ 返程票   ⑫ 登机口

⑬ 普通舱   ⑭ 登机牌

2. Complete the following dialogue in English with the information given.

(A＝the tour leader   B＝the tour guide)

A: Now, we're ready.

B: ① _____? (大家都退房了吗?)

A: I think so.

B：②_____.（请确认没有落下任何东西）

A：OK. You've been a great help to us in the past two weeks. Thank you very much.

B：③_____.（我很乐意那样做）

A：You are a part of our happy memories in China, really.

B：④_____.（跟你们相处我也感觉很高兴。真心祝愿你们回程平安愉快）

A：Thank you. I hope I can come to China again.

B：⑤_____.（希望你再到北京来）

A：I sure will, maybe with my family. Let's keep in touch.

B：⑥_____.（当然，请向您的家人转达我衷心的问候）

A：Definitely. Once again. I thank you for your excellent work.

B：⑦_____.（谢谢您的夸奖）

A：You sure deserve it.

B：⑧_____.（啊，到你们进去的时间了，现在我们得道别了）

A：Oh, yes. Good-bye, my dear.

B：⑨_____.（再见，希望以后再见到你们）

3. Listen and fill in the blanks.

(G＝the guide　　T＝the tourist)

G：Hello, Mr. Brown. It is time for me to ___①___.

T：Yes, we have to. It is hard to tear myself away from you and your friendly people, but ___②___. I have to go back home soon. Thank you very much for your ___③___. I will always remember you.

G：I hope you will ___④_____.

T：I hope so. I am sure I will return soon. I will tell you a piece of good news. I was invited to be a visiting professor to teach at Hunan University for a year.

G：___⑤_____.

T：Good-bye. Please say hello to your family for me.

G：A happy ___⑥___ home.

T：Good-bye. See you next year.

4. Simulation.

Three students are to play the roles of a local guide, a tourist leader, and a tourist member. Sunny, the guide from China International Travel Service, is seeing the tourists off at the airport. Explain what they are supposed to do.

◇ **Related Knowledge**

1. Preparations for a guide before departure from the group.

① Check the names, number of the tourists and the return tickets. If the group is going to leave the country by plane, the local guide should help the overseas tour leader confirm the air tickets.

② Confirm the time for the delivery of luggage with the porter and the tour leader, and then inform the tourists of the time.

③ Confirm the time for the morning call and breakfast. Fix the leaving time with the driver and the tour leader, and then inform the tourists.

④ Remind the tourists to pay their bills before they leave the hotel, and return the tourists' identity cards or passports.

2. A good farewell speech for seeing off tourists.

Seeing off tourists is the last step of the work of a tour guide. A good ending will give a great impression to the guests. To guide a tour group successfully, a guide must try to create a good first impression on his/her tourists. Therefore, you must make a full preparation beforehand. You should be prepared to deliver a farewell speech in a friendly, gracious, and sincere manner and handle problems enthusiastically and efficiently. Meanwhile, you must be mentally ready to face complaints from tourists.

During the seeing off, a guide must try to move the tourists with a pleasant personality. Also, you must be able to coordinate well with the tourists, and do everything you can to help all the guests. Try to make everyone a wonderful trip and give a great impression to them.

The most important thing of seeing off is to deliver a farewell speech. You should do it as follows.

(1) Opening remark.

The guide can quote poems about departure or friendship.

(2) Saying goodbye.

So it is time to say goodbye to you, although I hate to.

But every time I say goodbye, I find it hard to express myself.

(3) Expressing thanks.

It is really my pleasure to have been with you all in the past days.

First of all, thank you for your great interest in Chinese culture.

(4) Reviewing the tour.

We have had a great time together seeing...

Besides we went to...

We watched...

(5) Eliciting a response.

Can you remember what they are?

Yes,... and...

Right, although the story is... We see the beauty of...

What other places did we go then?

Exactly. We also went to..., isn't it?

(6) Wishing for keeping contact.

I would like to make friends with you all. So please call me or email me if you need any help. If you come to... I will happy to show you more about the beauty of real...

(7) Making a sincere apology.

By the way, I would like to make a sincere apology for any inconvenience if we weren't able to satisfy some of your needs despite all our efforts. Your comments and suggestions are warmly welcome and will assist us in continuously improving our service.

(8) Express good wishes.

Last but not least, goodbye is the moment to start to miss each other. So I hope you all will have a pleasant journey back home, and look forward to meeting you again.

3. A Sample of a farewell Speech.

Ladies and gentlemen:

Your current visit to China is drawing to a close. I would like to say a few words before you leave this country, though I am not a speechmaker.

Seventeen days have elapsed so quickly and you have visited several cities in our country. Examples of these are Beijing, which is the capital of the People's Republic of

China; Xi'an, the paradise of archeologists both at home and abroad; Chengdu, the capital of Sichuan Province, which is the land of heavenly gift; Chongqing, which will become the largest city in China; Wuhan, the birth place of Chu Culture; Kunming of Yunnan Province is a charming place, spring hovers all the year round, and flowers of all sorts bloom in a riot of color. Then we flew to Guilin which claims to be "second to none" in scenery. The Li River cruise was superb. Finally we came to Shanghai which people used to call the adventures' paradise before 1949. Everybody in the group has been very cooperative, friendly and supportive. That is what I witnessed and experienced as a national guide. It was much appreciated.

A Chinese saying goes, "A friend from afar brings boundless joy." Parting is such sweet sorrow. Happy to meet, sorry to depart, and happy to meet again.

Now, we are at the parking lot of the airport. I'd like to wish you bon voyage and please give my best regards to your families. Thank you and wish you all the best!

4. Tips for seeing off guests.

(1) A tour guide might feel exhausted after a day's work, but she/he has to take responsibility for settling down farewell issues. The following steps are suggested to improve work efficiency.

◆ Make the ways of departure clear.

◆ Confirm flight tickets with the tour leader or guests themselves if departing by plane, or confirm the number of the train/ship, departure time, and station if leaving by train or other transportation.

◆ Confirm luggage quota allowed.

◆ Calculate the time needed for the ride from the hotel to the airport/train station. Extra time must be considered to avoid possible rush in a traffic jam. If necessary, consult the driver for time needed.

(2) To ensure a perfect departure arrangement, a tour guide is encouraged to observe the following issues.

◆ Contact the bus driver and arrange related bus-renting issues.

◆ Inform the tourists of all necessary information at least one day earlier.

◆ If the guests leave very early in the morning, an early check-out should be scheduled. If possible, a take-out breakfast should be arranged.

◆ Arrive a little bit earlier than the meeting time to provide necessary assistance.

◆ Remind the tourists to take all their belongings and travel documents before leaving the hotel.

◆ Give clear instructions on airport check-in and customs declaration, and provide necessary assistance if needed or requested.

◆ Give friendly smiles and good wishes when saying farewell.

5. Useful sentences.

(1) A farewell speech.

◇ How time flies!

◇ Your current visit to Shanghai is drawing to a close.

◇ We thank you for coming.

◇ We would thank you again for your great patience, cooperation and understanding, which have made our job easier.

◇ The tour couldn't have been that successful without your support.

◇ It is a good banquet that does not end.

◇ I hope you have enjoyed all your stay.

◇ Bon voyage!

◇ Could you fill out this form of evaluation for me?

◇ I'd like to express our heartfelt gratitude to you for your efforts and excellent service.

◇ I would like to welcome you back.

(2) Seeing guests off at the airport.

◇ Here we are at the airport.

◇ Would you please wait for me for a few seconds?

◇ It's time for us to say goodbye to each other.

◇ Thank you for all your kindness.

◇ A happy journey home.

Keys for Reference

Module 1 Travel Information

Task 1 Recommending Tourism Products

1. Please choose the correct words for the sentences.

① tour　②agency　③ group　④ depart　⑤ accommodation

3. Listen and fill in the blanks.

(1) Complete the dialogue.

① How may I help you

② Changsha to spend my holiday

③ two-day tour package

④ every weekend

⑤ free time in the first evening

⑥ 800 Yuan

⑦ transportation, accommodate, meals and entry to the tourist sites

⑧ this weekend

⑨ Just me

⑩ Kevin Li

⑪ 0107635298

⑫ a two-day-one-night group tour to Changsha in the name of Kevin Li this weekend

(2) Listen again and check true (T) or false (F) for each statement.

① F

② T

③ T

④ F

⑤ F

⑥ T

Script:

A: Good morning. How may I help you?

B: Good morning. I'd like to go to Changsha to spend my holiday. Could you recommend a two-day tour package for me?

A: Sure. We have a tour package to Changsha every weekend. Here is the brochure.

B: That's fine. Is there free time for shopping?

A: Yes. You will have free time in the first evening.

B: That's good. I will take this tour. How much is it?

A: 800 Yuan. Including fees and tickets of transportation, accommodate, meals and entry to the tourist sites.

B: OK. I want to book one for this weekend.

A: How many people are there in your party?

B: Just me.

A: May I know your name and telephone number, please?

B: Kevin Li, and you can call me at 0107635298.

A: OK. Let me confirm your reservation. You have booked a two-day-one-night group tour to Changsha in the name of Kevin Li this weekend. If there is no problem, please pay 800 Yuan.

B: OK.

Task 2 Answering Tourists' Queries

1. Complete the dialogue.

① How can I help you?

② How many people are there in your group?

③ How long would you like to stay?

④ Please have a look at our brochure.

⑤ The charges include the round-trip tickets, fees for two nights accommodation, three meals a day and entry to the tourist sites.

⑥ Do you have a discount?

⑦ The price can be lower if there are more than four people in your group.

⑧ You can call us to confirm your reservation.

3. Listen and fill in the blanks.

(1) Listen to the first part and answer the questions.

① Beijing.   ② Three.   ③ Nov. 12.   ④ 15,000 pounds.   ⑤ Four.

(2) Listen to the second part and decide whether the statements are true (T) or false (F).

① T   ② F   ③ T

(3) Listen to the third part and complete the dialogue.

① a five-day-four-night tour to Beijing from Nov. 12—Nov. 14 for 2 adults and 1 child

② 10,000 pounds deposit

③ How would you like to pay, by cash or credit card

④ We accept Visa, Master Card, Amex, Diners Club and JCB

⑤ Please sign here

⑥ This is your copy of reservation form and receipt

⑦ Hope you have a nice journey

Scripts:

Part One

A: Good morning. I'd like to know your tour package to Beijing.

B: How many people are there in your group?

A: Three. My husband, daughter and me.

B: OK. How long would you like to stay in Beijing?

A: About 5 days.

B: When would you like to go?

A: Our holiday is from Nov. 11—Nov. 17.

B: Fine. There is a 5-day-4-night tour package to Beijing from Nov. 12—Nov. 16. Is it alright?

A: Let me have a look. That's good. How much is it?

B: 6,000 pounds per adult and 3,000 pounds for a child from 6 to 14.

A: OK. I will reserve this one.

Part Two

B: May I know your name and contact number please?

A: Anna Stone. 13765298308

B: By the way. How old is your daughter?

A: She is 10 years old.

B: Please complete the reservation form and sigh here.

A: OK, here you are.

Part Three

B: OK. Mrs. Stone. You reserved a five-day-four-night tour to Beijing from Nov. 12—Nov. 14 for 2 adults and 1 child. You have to pay 10,000 pounds deposit.

A: No problem.

B: How would you like to pay, by cash or credit card?

A: Credit card.

B: We accept Visa, Master Card, Amex, Diners Club and JCB.

A: I have a Master Card. Here you are.

B: Thank you. Please sign here.

A: OK.

B: This is your copy of reservation form and receipt. Please keep them well.

A: Thank you very much.

B: Hope you have a nice journey.

Module 2   Receiving Tasks

Task 1   Familiar with the Plan

2. Phrases interpreting.

带团委托书	certificate of a package tour	单人间	single room
全陪	national guide	中国国际旅行社	CITS (China International Travel Service)
接待计划	reception plan	入境	immigration
地陪	local guide	始发站	departure station
标准间	standard room	终点站	terminal station

3. Listen and fill in the blanks.

① keep up   ② background information.

③ warehouses and storehouses.   ④ a property developer

⑤ recreation   ⑥ outdoor activities

⑦ nature reserve   ⑧ man-made features

⑨ 12 meters high   ⑩ take advantage of

Script：

Welcome to all of you...can everybody see and hear me? Good... I'm Sally, your guide for this tour of the Bicentennial Park... I hope that you're all wearing your most comfortable shoes and that you can keep up the pace. So let's get under way on our tour around this wonderful park. I'll start today with some general background information. There used to be a lot of factories in this area until the 1960s. Creating the park required demolition of lots of derelict buildings on the site, so most of the exciting park space all around you was originally warehouses and storehouses. The idea of building a public park here was first discussed when a property developer proposed a high-rise housing development, but the local community wasn't happy.

If the land was to be cleaned up, they wanted to use the site for recreation. Residents wanted open space for outdoor activities, rather than housing or even an indoor sports complex. Now to the Bicentennial Park itself. It has two areas, a nature reserve and a formal park with man-made features and gardens. The tall blue-and-white building in front of us is called The Tower and is the central point for the formal gardens. It stands 12 meters high, so follow me up the stairs to where we can take advantage of the fantastic views. Well, here we are at the top of The Tower, and we're going to look at the view from each direction.

Task 2　Reconfirm the Arrangement

1. Listen and fill in the blanks.

① deluxe　　　　　　　② available

③ period　　　　　　　④ charge

⑤ current　　　　　　　⑥ possible

⑦ preferred　　　　　　⑧ pick-up

⑨ representative　　　　⑩ expected

Script:

R: Beijing Hotel. Reservation Desk. Can I help you?

G: I'm calling from New York. I'd like to reserve a room in your hotel.

R: What kind of room would you like, sir? We have single rooms, double rooms, suites and deluxe suites.

G: I'd like to book a double room from October 1 to October 7.

R: Would you like breakfast?

G: No, thanks.

R: Hold on please. I'll check if there is a room available for those days.

G: OK.

R: Sorry to have kept you waiting, sir. We'll have rooms available in that period.

G: How much do you charge for a double room?

R: The current rate is $120 per night.

G: OK. I'll take it. By the way, I'd like to have a quiet room if possible.

R: A quiet room is preferred. Could you give me your name, please?

G: George Smith. S-M-I-T-H.

R: Thank you, Mr. Smith. And what time will you be arriving, Mr. Smith?

G: Around 6:00 p.m. Do you have a pick-up service?

R: We have an airport representative to receive our guests there.

G: Oh, that's good.

R: Well, Mr. Smith. A double room without breakfast from October 1 to October 7. Am I right, Mr. Smith?

G: Yes, thank you.

R: Thank you for calling, Mr. Smith. You'll be expected to be here then. Good-bye.

2. Complete the following dialogue and then play the roles in pairs.

① I am Mary, the guide from China International Travel Service.

② Would you please pick up our 10 guests from Australia at 4 p.m. tomorrow at the Beijing airport on time?

③ I'd like to confirm whether the microphone and air conditioning on the bus are OK.

④ They will stay in Beijing for a five-day visit. And they will leave Beijing airport at 4 p.m. tomorrow for Beijing International Hotel. After a short rest, they will have dinner at half past six in the evening. Do you have any questions?

Task 3 Preparations for Meeting a Tour Group

1. Match each picture below with its word or phrase.

① e   ② c   ③ a   ④ b   ⑤ f   ⑥ d

3. Translation.

文化习惯、文化差异、当地礼仪和风俗：即使你怀着良好的意愿，这些文化陷阱也可能让你的旅行险象环生。从问候到饮食，稍不留神就会出差错，不仅让自己难堪，还有可能冒犯东道主。一旦你踏上异国的土地，就要对当地人的一举一动高度敏感。千万不要大惊小怪，尽量使自己泰然自若，对一些看似无礼的行为也不要恼火——比如插队。毕竟，我们生活在一个地球村，不同的文化构成了我们共同的家园。

Module 3 Immigration and Customs

Task 1 Check in at the Airport

1. Please write down the language in each corresponding task.

Tasks	Language
Explain to the tourists whose luggage is overweight. Tell them clearly how the airline charges for excess weight.	① I'm sorry that our free allowance is 35 kilograms, but these three suitcases excess the weight. ② We have to charge you 50 dollars for this one that excesses 5 kilos, 60 dollars for that one that excesses 6 kilos and 30 dollars for the baggage that is only 3 kilos overweight.
Tell the counter clerk that the tourists' special request.	By the way, three members said that they have ordered vegetarian meals at your web.
Check the board gate and the flying time with the clerk.	Hello Miss, we are a group of 35 people going to China by Flight HM 268.
After checking in, ask the tourists to receive their passports.	Now we've already checked-in. Please collect your passport here and keep it well.

3. Fill in the blanks with the right words according to the recording.

① confirm   ② boarding passes   ③ meal   ④ baggage   ⑤ seating

Script:

Online Check-in

Online check-in is the process in which passengers confirm their presence on a flight through the Internet and print their own boarding passes. Depending on the specific flight, passengers may also enter details such as meal options and baggage quantities and select their preferred seating.

Task 2 Go through the Immigration

1. Fill in the arrival card.

FULL NAME (AS APPEARS IN PASSPORT): Susan Beckham	
PASSPORT NO.: GS108756	
DATE OF EXPIRY(DD-MM-YYYY): 08-12-1991	SEX: MALE FEMALE √
PLACE OF ISSUE: London	
NATIONALITY: British	
CITY OF RESIDENCE: Edinburgh	
COUNTRY OF RESIDENCE: United Kingdom	
LAST PLACE OF EMBARKATION: Beijing	
FLIGHT NO.: HM268	

2. Listen to a flight announcement and fill in the blanks.

① attention ② extraordinary ③ clearing ④ delayed

⑤ supply ⑥ inform ⑦ cooperation

Script:

Ladies and gentlemen, attention please. Because of extraordinary odd weather, we have to wait for snow clearing, our flight will be delayed for about an hour. Now we will supply beverages/dinner/snack. We will inform you of further details as soon as possible. Thanks for your understanding and cooperation.

3. Fill in the blanks with the words given below.

① Prohibited ② smuggler ③ non-smoking ④ items ⑤ dutiable ⑥ tax

Task 3 Go through the Customs

1. Listen to the paragraph and fill in the blanks.

① foreign ② particular ③ purpose ④ business ⑤ investigation

Script:

Visa

Visa is an official mark put on a passport by representatives of the foreign country. It gives holders permission to enter, pass through or leave a particular country. There are different types of visa according to the purpose of visiting the country, including on education, on business, for traveling, for investigation, for visiting relatives, etc.

3. Translation from Chinese to English.

① I bring some gifts to my friends. By the way, I bought a bottle of perfume on the flight.

② Please eat up all the imported fruits before leaving the custom. Otherwise I have to confiscate them according to the rule.

③ If you have anything to declare, please fill in the declaration form first and go through the red channel.

④ According to the US Customs requirement, you need not pay tax for a gift within 10 dollars.

⑤ Sometimes the customs would ask you to register the foreign currency that you carry around.

Module 4   Meeting Guests

Task 1   Meet the tour group

1. Match each picture below with the words or phrases.

① b   ② f   ③ a   ④ c   ⑤ e   ⑥ d

2. Interpret the phrases.

问询处	inquiry office; information counter	一行25人	a party of twenty five
导游证	tour guide certificate / the certificate of tour guide	机场班车	shuttle bus
导游旗	tour flag	行李箱	suitcase
接站牌	welcome board	领队	tour leader
地陪	local guide	走失	get lost

3. Discuss and write.

① If you are a local guide, what should you do to fully prepare for meeting a tour group?

First: I must wear my tour guide ID card and take the schedule of the tour group.

Second: I should accomplish the required formalities in the travel agency.

Third: I should take a tour banner if I take a group of more than 10 members.

Finally: I should take a copy of the insurance policies, various vouchers, the travel schedule and a loudspeaker.

② What can you do to make yourself easily visible to your guests at the airport or at the railway station?

Stand at a highly visible place at the station exit, indicate the group name and number, the leader's name or the national guide's name on the meeting board, and lift the meeting board for the guests.

4. Listen and fill in the blanks.

① aren't you Miss Mary Smith

② Oh, I'm terribly sorry

③ Excuse me, Madam, are you Miss Mary Smith from New Zealand

④ I'm your local guide, Lin Yang. I'm from Fuzhou Comfort Travel Service

⑤ And could you tell me if everyone in your group is here

⑥ we will need to make some changes in room and restaurant arrangements

⑦ may I have the baggage check, Miss Smith

⑧ I'll see to it that it goes to our hotel as soon as possible

⑨ Please tell the group to follow this little green banner

⑩ go ahead

Script:

A: Excuse me, Madam, aren't you Miss Mary Smith?

C: No, I am not. I'm afraid you've made a mistake.

A: Oh, I'm terribly sorry.

C: That's all right.

A: Excuse me, Madam, are you Miss Mary Smith from New Zealand?

B: Yes, I am.

A: I'm your local guide, Lin Yang. I'm from Fuzhou Comfort Travel Service. How do you do, Miss Smith?

B: How do you do, Miss Lin? Thank you for meeting us.

A: I'm glad to be of service, Miss Smith. Welcome to Fuzhou. And could you tell me if everyone in your group is here?

B: I'm sorry to say one man didn't come for business reasons. We now have 21 people including me.

A: That's all right. However, we will need to make some changes in room and restaurant arrangements.

B: Sorry to cause you trouble.

A: No trouble. Now, may I have the baggage check, Miss Smith?

B: Of course. Here you are. There are 16 pieces altogether. Will we have our luggage once we reach the hotel?

A: I'll see to it that it goes to our hotel as soon as possible.

B: I'm glad to hear that. Shall we go now?

A: Yes, of course. Please tell the group to follow this little green banner.

B: Sure. You go ahead and we'll follow.

Task 2 Meet a FIT guest

1. Discuss and write down.

What travel agencies do you know? Please write down at least 5 travel agencies' names.

China International Travel Service (CITS)中国国际旅行社(国旅)

China Travel Service/Agency (CTS/CTA)中国旅行社(中旅)

China Youth Travel Service (CYTS)中国青年旅行社(中青旅)

China Comfort Travel Service 中国康辉旅行社

Overseas Chinese Travel Service (OCTS)中国海外旅行社/华侨旅行社

Shanghai Spring and Autumn International Travel Service (Spring Tour)

Hunan Enjoy Going International Travel Service (Enjoy Goning)

Hunan Huatian International Travel Service (Huatian Travel)

CITIC Travel Corporation

New Century Tourism Co., Ltd

2. Discuss and make a dialogue.

When you meet with a foreign guest for the first time, how to chat with her/him? Try to make a dialogue about chatting with an unfamiliar guest.

① Greeting. (Hi. Nice to meet you. How are you?)

② Talking about the weather. (It's a sunny day, isn't it?)

③ Talking about the trip. (Where are you from? Are you here on vacation or on business? How long have you been in China? How do you like China?)

④ Talking about Chinese. (Can you speak Chinese? I can help you with Chinese if you like.)

⑤ Say goodbye. (I'm sorry, I'm afraid I have to go now. Oh, nice talking with you.)

⑥ Do not refer to any sensitive or private things like politics, religion belief, age, marital status, etc.

Dialogue Sample

A: Hi, nice to meet you.

B: Glad to see you.

A: How are you?

B: Fine, and you?

A: Not bad.

B: It's a sunny day, isn't it?

A: Yes, I like this kind of weather.

B: Where are you from?

A: I'm from Canada.

B: Canada is a beautiful country.

A: Have you been to Canada?

B: Unfortunately, no. I learnt that from textbooks and television. How long have you been in China?

A: I just arrived last week.

B: Are you here on vacation or on business?

A: I'm on a business trip.

B: How do you like China?

A: I like it, especially Chinese people and Chinese food.

B: Can you speak Chinese?

A: Unfortunately, no. /Just a little.

B: I can help you with Chinese if you like.

A: That's very nice of you. Thank you.

3. Look at the photos showing meeting tasks. Then fill in the blanks with verbs to complete the description of the tasks.

① Confirm   ② Contact

③ Bring   ④ Guarantee

⑤ stand   ⑥ Look for

⑦ counting   ⑧ lead

⑨ Confirm   ⑩ Head

4. Listen and fill in the blanks.

① that's right

② I'm the guide from Pacific Tour Agency

③ looking for

④ I'm always at your service

⑤ come this way

⑥ Did you have a pleasant trip

⑦ Not bad

⑧ get you to the hotel

⑨ eager to

⑩ looking forward to

Script:

(A: Lucy   B: Mr. Smith)

A: Good evening, sir. Are you Mr. Smith from England?

B: Ah, yes, that's right.

A: Glad to meet you, Mr. Smith. I'm the guide from Pacific Tour Agency. My name is Lucy. Welcome to China.

B: Hello, I was just looking for the guide.

A: I'm always at your service, sir. Would you please come this way please? The coach is waiting outside. Did you have a pleasant trip?

B: Not bad. But I've made too many flights these days. I could hardly remember how many take-offs and landings I've been through these two days.

A: So, we must get you to the hotel as soon as possible. I've already made a reservation for you.

B: Wonderful. I'm eager to take a shower as soon as possible.

A: I hope to see you refreshed and revitalized tomorrow morning, as we are going to visit the Great Wall.

B: I' sure I will. Actually, we are looking forward to seeing the great wonder in the world.

Module 5　On the Way to the Hotel

Task 1　Extending a welcome speech

1. When traveling, how would you like the tour guide and the journey? Please use adjectives to describe.

The guide: on time, warm, friendly, careful, enthusiastic

The journey: rewarding, interesting, unforgettable, pleasant, fantastic, smooth, comfortable, enjoyable, safe

2. Interpret the phrases.

致辞	extend a speech	舒适的	comfortable
背靠着椅子坐	sit back	愉快的	enjoyable
自我放松	relax yourself	合作	cooperation
随时为您服务	at your service at anytime	提前	in advance
确保,一定	be sure	感激	appreciate

3. Please write down the languages can be used in the corresponding tasks.

Tasks	Language
On behalf of the travel agency, the guide welcome the tourists	Good afternoon, ladies and gentlemen. Welcome to Hunan.
Tell the tourists the guide's name and the travel agency	I am Simon, your local guide from Hunan China International Travel Service.
Introduce the driver	This is Mr. Li, our driver, who has 10 years of driving experience.
Express sincere desire to serve the tourists	During your stay here, I will be at your service at anytime and do everything possible to make your trip comfortable and enjoyable.
Wish the tourists a good journey	Wish you a nice trip.

4. Listen and fill in the blanks.

① philosopher　② joy　③ behalf　④ agencies

⑤ warmest　⑥ distinguished　⑦ satisfy　⑧ experience

⑨ understanding　⑩ shapes

Script:

Confucius, our ancient great philosopher once said, "What a great joy it is to have friends from afar." Today, with such great joy, on behalf of China International Travel Service, Beijing, one of the largest and best travel agencies in China, I'd like to extend our warmest welcome to all of you, our distinguished guests from the other side of the Pacific.

I also hope that during your short stay in Beijing, you not only can satisfy your eyes and stomach, but also experience the real Chinese culture and have a better understanding of the Chinese people and its ongoing reforms, which shapes the greatness of China.

Task 2　Adjusting the time difference

1. When it is 8 a.m. in China, what's the time in the following cities? Please write down.

City	Time		City	Time
Tokyo	9		Berlin	1
Seoul	9		Paris	1
Bangkok	7		New York	19(the previous day)
Singapore	8		Sydney	10
London	0		Male	5

2. Interpret the phrases.

北京标准时间	Beijing Standard Time	时区	time zone
时差	time difference	适应时差	adjust to the time difference
遭受	suffer from	时差带来的不良感受或反应	jet lag
当地时间	local time	东半球	Eastern Hemisphere
晚于	later than	早于	early than
在……之后	behind	在……的前面	ahead of

3. Try to translate the following sentences.

① What's the time difference between Tokyo and London?

② Beijing is 8 hours earlier than London.

③ We are on Beijing time.

④ 我从来没什么时差的困扰。

⑤ 我总有时差不良反应。

4. Listen and fill in the blanks.

① inform   ② advance   ③ on time   ④ make sure

⑤ time difference   ⑥ traveling   ⑦ Standard   ⑧ current

⑨ adjust   ⑩ confusion

Script：

We will always inform you in advance when we will meet to go somewhere and when we will have our meals. It's very important that you always try to be on time. To make sure that we don't have any problems, I'd like to remind you of the time difference. While you are traveling in China, you will always use Beijing Standard Time. Right now it is September 20th and the current time is 10:00 a.m. Please adjust your watches now, so that we can avoid any confusion later on.

Task 3 Guiding on the Way

1. Please match the tourist attractions with the corresponding pictures.

   ① g   ② e   ③ i   ④ a   ⑤ c   ⑥ b   ⑦ h   ⑧ f   ⑨ d

2. Interpret the phrases.

音量适中	moderate volume	第二大	second-largest
五星级酒店	a five-star hotel	与……接界,毗邻	border
一瞥,一看	glimpse	旅游胜地	tourist attraction
郊区	outskirt	当提到……	when it comes to
高速公路	expressway	烹饪,风味	cuisine
期望	look forward to	县	county
开发区	development zone	世界自然遗产	world natural heritage
荣誉,名声	reputation	一线明星	A-lister

3. Listen and fill in the blanks.

   ① common   ② skill   ③ thinking   ④ English-speaking

   ⑤ frightened   ⑥ irrelevant   ⑦ look   ⑧ voice

   ⑨ pace   ⑩ eye contact

   Script:

   A tour guide should first have the common language that his customers use. When you have the sufficient language skill, your customers will feel that they can share the atmosphere easily.

   Language plays an important part in a culture. One's cultural background determines his thinking style. Our native language is Chinese, so our thinking style is different from the English-speaking people. You need to practice the corresponding language until you can use it to the satisfaction of your tourists.

   Being a tour guide, one will have a lot of chances to talk in public. So you need public speaking skill. If you are so frightened when you stand up, it is not very good because nobody wants to see a frightened face with irrelevant manners. You are required to look at the listeners evenly; your voice should be clear and loud enough for everybody to hear. Your pace of speaking is as important as your volume, because if you talk too fast, people cannot follow. Additionally, your facial expression, gesture, posture and eye contact will all help the listener to understand you.

4. Complete the dialogue.

① Is everybody here

② I will be your local guide during your stay in Beijing

③ Mr. Zhou is a responsible and experienced driver

④ We highly appreciate your understanding and cooperation

⑤ You might as well have a look at the city along the way

⑥ You must be very tired after the long trip

⑦ one of the largest squares in the world today

⑧ That grand building contains two museums

⑨ To the south of the monument is the Chairman Mao Memorial Hall

⑩ Let's get off and go to the reception desk

Task 4　Warm reminding

2. Interpret the phrases.

提醒	remind	车牌号码	bus number
遵守时间安排	be punctual	犹豫	hesitate
保持健康	stay healthy	好好照顾	take a good care of
20人的团队	a group of 20	个人物品	personal belongings
自来水	tap water	手机号码	mobile number/phone number

3. Try to translate the following sentences.

① During your stay in Hunan, I'd like to remind you of four important things.

② The weather in spring is changeable. Please take a coat with you when going out.

③ Please always take a good care of your personal belongings.

④ 为了避免不必要的问题，旅游期间请务必准时。

⑤ 我的手机会24小时开机，如有需要请随时打给我。

Module 6　At the Hotel

Task 1　Checking in

1. In what order will the following procedures be served in checking in?

d. b. f. a. g. e. c

2. Listening practice.

① A　　② A　　③ C　　④ D　　⑤ D

Script:

Guest: Hi. I have a reservation for tonight.

Hotel Clerk: And your name?

Guest: It's Nelson. Charles Nelson.

Hotel Clerk: Okay. Mr. Nelson. That's a room for five, and...

Guest: Excuse me? You mean a room for five dollars? I didn't know the special was so good.

Hotel Clerk: No, no, no. According to our records, a room for five guests was booked under your name.

Guest: No. No. Hold on. There must be some mistake.

Hotel Clerk: Okay. Let's check this again. Okay, Mr. Charles C. Nelson for tonight...

Guest: Ah. There's the problem. My name is Charles Nelson, not Charles C. Nelson. [Uh] You must have two guests under the name.

Hotel Clerk: Okay. Let me check this again. Oh. Okay. Here we are.

Guest: Yeah.

Hotel Clerk: Charles Nelson. A room for one for the 19th...

Guest: Wait, wait! It was for tonight. Not tomorrow night.

Hotel Clerk: Hum. Hum. I don't think we have any rooms for tonight. There's a convention going on in town, and uh, let's see. Yeah, no rooms.

Guest: Ah come on! You must have something. Anything.

Hotel Clerk: Well. We do have some rooms under renovation with just a roll-away bed. [Uh] None of the normal amenities like a TV or working shower or toilet.

Guest: Ah man. Come on. There must be something else.

Hotel Clerk: Well. Let, let me check my computer here. Ah!

Guest: What?

Hotel Clerk: There has been a cancellation for this evening. A honeymoon suite is now available.

Guest: Great. I'll take it.

Hotel Clerk: But I'll have to charge you two hundred fifty dollars for the night.

Guest: Ah. Man. I should get a discount for the inconvenience.

Hotel Clerk: Well. The best I can give you is a ten percent discount plus a ticket for a free continental breakfast.

Guest: Hey. Isn't the breakfast free anyway?

Hotel Clerk: Well, only on weekends.

Guest: I want to talk to the manager.

Hotel Clerk: Wait, wait, wait, Mr. Nelson. I think I can give you an additional 15 percent discount and I'll throw in a free room for the next time you visit us.

Guest: That will be a long time.

3. Fill in the blanks.

① checked ② rate ③ signature ④ filled ⑤ reservation

⑥ confirmation ⑦ deliver ⑧ registration ⑨ assist ⑩ schedule

4. Match.

① ask for ② fill with ③ in advance ④ check out ⑤ either or

Task 2 Introducing Hotel Facilities

1. Match the hotel terms with the correct Chinese.

① O C ② F R ③ B N

④ Q I ⑤ E D ⑥ M G

2. Reading practice.

(1) ① F   ② T   ③ T   ④ F

3. Complete the following dialogue.

① There is an inside swimming-pool on the first floor

② play baseball and bowling etc

③ Is there a beauty salon and a souvenir shop?

④ a brochure of the hotel

⑤ Internet café

⑥ Internet access

Task 3   Wake-up Call

1. Match the words in Column A with the English equivalents in Column B:

a. F   b. C   c. B   d. A   e. D   f. I   g. J   h. H   i. E   j. G

Module 7   Talking about the Itinerary

Task 1   Discussing the Itinerary

1. Listen and fill in the blanks.

① itinerary   ② spare   ③ received   ④ changes   ⑤ go over

⑥ destination   ⑦ Exactly   ⑧ in advance   ⑨ hesitate   ⑩ wonderful

Text:

(Simon, from CITS, is discussing the itinerary with the tour group leader, Mr. Black.)

(S=Simon   B=Mr. Black)

S: Good evening, Mr. Black.

B: Good evening, Simon.

S: I've come to discuss your itinerary. Can you spare some time right now?

B: Sure. Our group received a copy of the itinerary before we came to China. Have there been any changes?

S：There have been no changes so far.

B：OK. Then let's go over the itinerary. We stay in Beijing for seven days. Then we go on to Chongqing for three days. Our last destination is Sichuan Province, where we stay for five days. The whole trip will last 15 days. Is that correct?

S：Exactly. If there are any changes, I'll let you know in advance.

B：Oh, that'd be great. Then we'll leave everything to you.

S：My pleasure. If you or any of your group members need any help at all, don't hesitate to ask. I hope you will have a wonderful time in China.

B：Thank you.

2. Special term.

(1) Put the following into English.

① selected itinerary

② add-ons

③ time for personal arrangements

④ special service requirements

⑤ group size

⑥ folk custom tour

⑦ trade observation tour

⑧ itinerary map

⑨ guest nights

⑩ extension of stay

(2) Put the following into Chinese.

① 国外派导游的旅游团

② 最终旅行路线

③ 全项委托

④ 最畅销的中国旅游路线

⑤ 娱乐或变换项目

⑥ 上岸参观

⑦ 预计抵达时间

⑧ 旅行安排

⑨ 中途小目的地

⑩ 观光旅行

3. Please fill in the blanks.

Yuelu Academy, Orange Island, Changsha Fire Palace Restaurant, the Museum of Hunan Province, the Xiang Embroidery Museum, Zan Feast Restaurant.

4. Decide whether the following statements are true (T) or false (F).

T F T T

5. Complete the following dialogue in English with the information given.

① Certainly

② Here is a tentative plan I drafted

③ Please take a look at it and let me know your opinion.

④ Should everything be slow and relaxing?

⑤ Shall I put off the wake-up call until 8:30?

⑥ If we get up late

⑦ we will probably not be able to visit some of the places in the plan

⑧ Then what are they interested in

⑨ and what shall we skip?

⑩ May I have a look at it?

⑪ That's not a difficult job for me

⑫ Here is my mobile number. Don't be hesitate to get in touch with me, if you run into problems.

Task 2 Handling the Changes in the Itinerary

1. Complete the following dialogue in English with the information given.

① now that you've finished with your check-in, shall we have a brief discussion about what we are going to do tomorrow and the day after?

② I planned to leave at 9:00. Is that all right?

③ As a native of Nanjing, I suggest you visit the Zhongshan tourist area for the first day of the trip.

④ For the morning, we will visit Sun Yat-sen's Mausoleum and Ming Tombs.

⑤ When it gets dark, we will have a walk in the Confucius Temple and taste some famous Qinhuai snacks.

⑥ However, I can promise you something unique in the Confucius Temple.

⑦ It's quite different from other Buddhist temples. It's worth visiting.

⑧ It ranks third in China, only behind Wangfujing in Beijing and Nanjing Road in Shanghai.

⑨ If you are interested in the history of China, the alternative is a visit to the former Office of President.

⑩ we will give up shopping then.

3. Translation.

① Before the arrival of a tour group, the local guide should study the reception program in detail and get enough information on the tour members so as to draft a tentative itinerary.

② A tour guide should abide by the accepted practice of "regarding tourists as supreme". It would be unwise and unacceptable for a tour guide to impose his/her personal interests upon his/her guests.

4. Fill in the blanks.

① features   ② informative   ③ location   ④ Day-by-day events

5. Listen and fill in the blanks.

① vacation   ② location   ③ length   ④ formulate

⑤ amazing   ⑥ suitable   ⑦ historical   ⑧ jackets

⑨ pants   ⑩ gathered   ⑪ destination   ⑫ in case

Text:

To plan a perfect vacation, you should keep in mind such matters as cost, location, and the length of stay.

First, choose where you aim to go for your vacation.

Then formulate your itinerary. Surf the Internet or read some books about amazing sites, places to visit, and things to do. Make sure you book suitable means of transportation for the right dates.

Write down all the possible sites and choose those that suit you best. Older travelers may prefer to visit historical sites, while young people may like to visit shopping centers.

Get the right clothing ready for your holiday. If you are going to somewhere hot you may need shorts and T-shirts, but if you are going to a colder place you need to pack jackets and warm pants.

Once you have chosen where you wish to go, you can now decide how you are going to get around—by car, taxi, train, plane, bus, or boat.

After you have gathered all the information, find a map of your destination to help you get around.

Write down all the information you have gathered in case you forget.

Module 8　At the Restaurant

Task 1　Meet the Tour Group

1. Matching.

① C　　② E　　③ D　　④ B　　⑤ A　　⑥ F

2. Phrases interpreting.

准确人数	precise number	一行 21 人	a group of twenty-one people
餐馆前台	receptionist	餐桌预订	booking tables
旅行社	travel agency	菜单	menu
到达时间	time of arrival	提前	in advance

4. Listen and fill in the blanks.

① Can I help you

② book some tables for 21 people

③ What time is it for

④ not booked

⑤ How long is the wait

⑥ make

⑦ May I have your name, please

⑧ by the window

⑨ No problem

⑩ looking forward

Text:

A waiter is receiving a telephone call from a local guide to book a table for tonight.

(G=Guide　　W=Waiter)

W: Good morning. Century Restaurant. Can I help you?

G: I'd like to book some tables for 21 people, please.

W: What time is it for?

G: Around 7:00 p.m.

W: I'm sorry sir, we are not booked for 7:00, but would you mind some waiting?

G: How long is the wait?

W: Eight o'clock should be OK.

G: OK, please make it at eight.

W: May I have your name, please?

G: Steven. By the way, we'd like a table by the window.

W: No problem, Mr. Brown. We're looking forward to having you with us tonight. Thank you for calling.

G: Goodbye!

W: Goodbye!

Task 2 Dining at a Chinese restaurant

1. Matching.

① B   ② A   ③ D   ④ C

2. Discuss and write down.

What are the table manners in a Chinese restaurant?

① When you go to the table, you should wait for the elders to sit down firstly.

② Never stick your chopsticks on your bowl, and lay them on your dish instead.

③ When your mouth is full of food, do not talk with any others. You should chew your food gently and elegantly.

3. Discuss and make a dialogue.

When you lead foreign guests to a Chinese restaurant for the first time, how to introduce to them? Try to make a dialogue about it.

(G=the guide   V=the visitor)

G: Good afternoon, welcome to China. Now, we will go to a Chinese restaurant. This restaurant has Hunan food, Sichuan food, and Beijing food. So, what kind of food would you like to try?

V: Yeah, now, we are in Changsha, I'd like to try some Hunan food.

G: Of course, would you like to eat spicy food or not?

V: Not spicy, thank you.

G: Yeah, this page is Hunan food. You can read this and make a choice.

V: OK, thank you very much.

G: It's my pleasure.

4. Listen and fill in the blanks.

① making you wait for so long

② Could you please wait us a little longer

③ have orange juice and tomato soup first

④ main dish

⑤ pork with salted vegetables

⑥ mushrooms

⑦ What special kind of desserts do you have

⑧ the soup and orange juice

Script:

A waiter is serving two visitors in a Chinese restaurant

Waiter: I'm sorry for making you wait for so long. This is menu. Are you ready to order now?

Tom: Sorry, we haven't decided yet. Could you please give us a little longer?

Waiter: No problem.

Tom: Well, I think I would like to have an orange juice and the tomato soup first. How about you, Jones.

Jones: The same for me, please.

Waiter: Yes, sir.

Jones: What main dish would you like, Tom?

Tom: Well, I'd like the pork with salted vegetable, please.

Jones: I'll have the mushroom.

Waiter: Would you like a dessert?

Jones: What special kind of desserts do you have?

Waiter: Lemon pie, hot cake in syrup, chocolate

Tom: Well, I think we'll order after we finish the main course.

Waiter: All right, I'll bring the soup and orange juice right away.

Task 3　Dining at a Western Restaurant

1. Matching.

① B　　② C　　③ D　　④ A

2. Discuss and write down.

What are the table manners in Western restaurants?

Firstly, you should try to keep up some kind of small talk with your neighbors now and then.

Secondly, when you are eating soup, the soup spoon is tipped slightly away from you.

Of course, you cannot make a noise by hitting the spoon against the plate.

3. Jack and Tim are deciding what to have for their meal. Try to make a dialogue about that.

J: What will you start with?

T: I don't know. I think I'll have soup.

J: It says they have tomato soup on the wall over there!

T: Great! I'll have tomato soup to start with.

J: What about the main course?

T: The meat dishes look good, but I think I prefer fish today. The baked fish looks good.

J: Great. What about dessert?

T: I'll decide on that later. Now what about you?

J: Um, yes, maybe I'll...

4. Listen and fill in the blanks.

① What can I do for you

② Do you have a reservation?

③ Are you ready to order now?

④ roast beef steak

⑤ How would you like your steak

Script:

A waiter is serving five visitors.

(V = the visitor   W = the waiter)

W: What can I do for you, sir?

V: I'd like a table for five.

W: Do you have a reservation?

V: Oh, I'm afraid not.

W: Well, this way, please. Are you ready to order now?

V: Yes. I'd like roast beef steak.

W: How would you like your steak, sir?

V: Well done, please.

W: Your order will be ready in 10 minutes.

V: Thank you.

Task 4 Tasting Local Food

1. Matching.

① D   ② A   ③ E   ④ F   ⑤ B   ⑥ C

2. Discuss and write down.
Make a five-minute speech to introduce Changsha local food.

Changsha local food is spicy, and a little acid. There are many special snacks, for example, Changsha-style stinky tofu, Changsha-style rice vermicelli, beer ducks and so on. It characterizes by thick pungent flavor, fresh aroma and deep color. Chilis, peppers and shallots are usually necessaries. And the common cooking techniques are stewing, frying, pot-roasting, braising and smoking.

3. Make a comment.

If it is the first time for you to taste Changsha local food, what comment will you make?

I think it is very delicious. Though it is a little acid and spicy, it catches my appetite.

4. Listen and fill in the blanks.

① many kinds of snacks

② have no famous name

③ your family and friends

④ steaming, frying, milling and other processes

⑤ unique traditional food

Script:

Snacks, snacks and more snacks. There are many kinds of snacks to choose from and most of them have no famous name and they are for tourists to bring home. I've just been out shopping and OK, here is a tip, well, I just learned that parched rice is very famous in Hunan Province. If you are looking for something for your family and friends, it is a good idea to get some. In fact, it is processed by steaming, frying, milling and other processes, and is unique traditional food.

Module 9　Sightseeing/Visiting Scenic Spots

Task 1　City Sightseeing

1. Special terms.

(1) Put the following into English.

① aquarium　　　　　　　　　② traditional culture

③ natural beauty　　　　　　　④ commercial district

⑤ industrial zone　　　　　　　⑥ Hi-Tech Development Zone

⑦ expressway　　　　　　　　⑧ flyover

⑨ underground　　　　　　　　⑩ children's playground

(2) Put the following into Chinese.

① 珠江三角洲　　　　　　　　② 林荫大道

③ 市政大厦　　　　　　　　　④ 旅游景点

⑤ 经济特区　　　　　　　　　⑥ 主题公园

⑦ 贸易港　　　　　　　　　　⑧ 基础设施

⑨ 海滨城市　　　　　　　　⑩ 铁路交通网

2. Complete the following dialogue.

① Would you wait for a minute

② keep them well

③ We will meet at the theatre at 5:30

④ Generally speaking, the park is a window on the world history, the world civilization and the world's tourist attractions as well

⑤ This is the Area of Asia. That is the Area of America.

⑥ Do you have a good time today

3. Translate the following sentences into English.

① Hanzhengjie Small Commodities Market is the largest collecting and distributing center and wholesale market dealing in commodities in Central China. Reasonable in price and complete in variety, the market attracts a large number of businessmen, customers and visitors from all over the country every day.

② Historically, Wuhan had been one of the "four well-known cities" in China. It boasts widespread business network and numerous circulating channels. A saying goes that "Any commodity will find a brisk market in Wuhan".

③ Chongqing is renowned as a "mountain city" because of its buildings on hillsides and mountains surrounding the city.

④ Wuhan is situated on the east edge of Jianghan Plain. Here the Changjiang River converges with the Han River, and thus the whole city is separated into three towns known as Wuchang, Hanyang and Hankou.

4. Listen and fill in the blanks.

① capital　　② consists　　③ urban　　④ Central　　⑤ hub

⑥ transportation　　⑦ reaches　　⑧ economy　　⑨ culture　　⑩ politics

Script:

Wuhan, the capital of Hubei Province, consists of the cities of Wuchang, Hankou and Hanyang with a total urban population of 10.91 million and an area of 8,494 square kilometers. As the largest city in Central China and the hub of land and water transportation on the middle reaches of the Yangtze River, Wuhan surely is the center of economy, culture, and politics in Central China and one of the most important cities in China.

Task 2　Cultural Landscape

1. Special terms.

(1) Put the following into English.

① the Palace Museum　　　　　　② Longmen Grottoes

③ the Terracotta Warriors and Horsed of Qin Shihuang

④ Giant Buddha of Leshan

⑤ Potala Palace　　　　　　　　⑥ Chairman Mao Memorial Hall

⑦ cultural relic　　　　　　　　⑧ No. 1 Pass under Heaven

⑨ the Temple of Heaven　　　　　⑩ Temple of Confucius

(2) Put the following into Chinese.

① 凯旋门　　　　　　　　　　　② 巴黎圣母院

③ 比萨斜塔　　　　　　　　　　④ 自由女神像

⑤ 时代广场　　　　　　　　　　⑥ 珍珠港

⑦ 好望角　　　　　　　　　　　⑧ 大都会艺术博物馆

⑨ 摄政大街　　　　　　　　　　⑩ 尼亚加拉瀑布

2. Complete the following dialogue.

① It is about 6,000 kilometers long

② beacon-fire towers

③ send smoke signals from the tower as an alarm

④ How high is it

⑤ an Chinese saying goes: "The man who doesn't reach the Great Wall is not a real man"

3. Translate the following sentences into English.

① The hall on the first floor is over 10 meters high. A huge fresco "White Clouds and Yellow Crane" stands inside the hall. The painting originates from the legendary story of "Drawing a Crane with an Orange Peel".

② The Terrace of Ancient Zither is by the side of the Moon Lake at the west foot of the Tortoise Hill in Hanyang. The familiar allusion of High Mountains and Flowing

Water, comes from here.

③ The chime bells excavated in Suizhou City of Hubei Province are known as one of the eight wonders of the ancient world.

④ Dujiang Weir, located about 57 kilometers northwest away from Chengdu, is a great ancient water conservancy project which was built in about 250 B. C.

⑤ The Forbidden City covers an area of 175 acres and is surrounded by a moat and a wall with a watch-tower on each corner.

5. Listen and fill in the blanks.

① Cultural tourism   ② customs   ③ architecture   ④ elements
⑤ particularly   ⑥ facilities   ⑦ museums   ⑧ revealing
⑨ festivals   ⑩ introduction   ⑪ features   ⑫ status
⑬ memorize   ⑭ beforehand   ⑮ comprehensively

Script:

Cultural tourism is travel related with a country or a region's culture, especially the customs of the local people, the history of the place, its art, architecture, religion, and other elements that have helped shape their way of life. Cultural tourism includes visiting urban areas, particularly historic or large cities and cultural facilities such as museums and theaters. It also includes tourism to rural areas revealing the traditions of the local people including festivals and rituals, etc.

A tour guide should provide cultural, historical and other information to tourists. Before the trip, the tour guide should prepare an introduction to the destination, which includes the history, location, features, its historical, national and international status, etc. The guide should memorize the introduction beforehand and interpret for visitors the cultural features of a location clearly and comprehensively during the trip.

Task 3 Natural Landscape

1. Listen and fill in the blanks.

① East Lake   ② Fairy Lake   ③ Wetland Park
④ give you a brief introduction to   ⑤ concept
⑥ swampland   ⑦ turf land   ⑧ naturally
⑨ artificially   ⑩ freshwater   ⑪ salt water

⑫ a mixture of fresh and salt water　　⑬ the kidney of the earth

⑭ one of the three ecosystems in the world

⑮ the other two are forest and the ocean

⑯ paradise of birds　　⑰ reptiles and mammalians

⑱ gene bank of species　　⑲ the Ramsar Convention

⑳ verified　　㉑ Birds Island　　㉒ Moon Island

㉓ ecopark　　㉔ red-crowned cranes

㉕ the Guardian Angles in Wetland

㉖ accounts for　　㉗ pleasant habitat

Script:

The water before us is a part of the East Lake, called the Fairy Lake. This lake is a must when you visit the Wetland Park. The wetland area for sightseeing accounts for two square kilometers, about 2 meters deep on average. I shall give you a brief introduction to the concept of a wetland. A wetland is a area of swampland or turf land. It is a water area that is naturally or artificially covered, for a short or long period of time, with freshwater, or salt water, or a mixture of fresh and salt water; a wetland is also a small part of the sea area. Its depth of water does not exceed six meters at low tide. As you know, the wetland is considered the Cradle of Life and the kidney of the earth. Being one of the three ecosystems in the world—the other two are forest and the ocean, the wetland is a paradise of birds, reptiles and mammalians, and it is also the gene bank of species. In 1971, the USA and other 36 countries signed the Ramsar Convention in Iran. China started to carry out items of the convention in an all-round way after 1994. On Dec. 12th, 2004, Xinghu Wetland Park, the first wetland park in China, was officially verified in the convention. Attention to both sides of the lake. On the lake are more than 20 islands. Birds Island and Moon Island are two of them. This island before us is the biggest ecopark for red-crowned cranes in South China. As you know, red-crowned cranes are considered the Guardian Angles in Wetland; there are more than 2,000 red-crowned cranes in the world, of which China accounts for more than 1,000. This park, with 50 red-crowned cranes, ranks the 4th of this kind in China. This park is also a pleasant habitat for other rare birds.

2. Put the following Chinese into English.

① Before departure, the local guide should arrive at the hotel 10 minutes earlier and wait for the tourists. After all tourists board the coach on time, he / she should count and check the number of the tourists. On the way to the tourist attraction, he/she would give an overview of the day's schedule and inform the group of any rules or regulations for the day's visit.

② When arriving at the scenic spot, the guide(he/she) should remind the tourists of the coach number, parking lot, and time for leaving. On entering the scenic spot, he/she should inform the group, in front of the tour map, of the tour route, time duration, meeting time and place. During the trip, the explanation of the local guide should be neither complicated nor simple.

③ Tour guides with good psychological qualities are enthusiastic and optimistic in their work. They are flexible, agile, cooperative, respectful, and impartial.

④ On the way back to the hotel, the local guide should do the following: give a brief overview of the day's tour, inform the group of the tour itinerary for the next day, remind the group of any rules or regulations, arrange for th wake-up call, and confirm the breakfast and the departure time.

Module 10　Transportation

Task 1　Public Transportation

1. Translate the sentences from Chinese to English.

① Please get off at the cinema.

② Here is the tip for you. / Keep the change.

③ You will have to transfer to Metro Line 1.

④ Could you tell me how to get to Tian'anmen Square?

⑤ Could you show me the nearest subway station?

3. Listen and fill in the blanks.

① 7:30 p.m.

② it is peak time now

③ could you find another way to the airport

④ Could you stop at the domestic departure gate of Terminal 2

⑤ 45 yuan

⑥ Please keep your change and receipt

⑦ Have a nice day

Script:

A: The plane will depart at 7:30 p.m. Could you hurry up?

B: I'm not sure, because it is peak time now. But I will try my best.

A: Well, could you find another way to the airport?

B: There is another way to the airport, but the distance is much more than this one. Do you mind to pay more?

A: No problem. I just worry about the time.

B: That's OK.

A: Could you stop at the domestic departure gate of Terminal 2?

B: OK. I'll go straight a little further.

A: Thank you. How much is it?

B: 45 yuan.

A: OK. Here is 50 yuan.

B: Thank you. Please keep your change and receipt.

A: Thank you.

B: Have a nice day.

Task 2 Rent a Car

1. Please write down the correct words based on the sentences.

① driving license

② pick up

③ insurance

④ SUV

⑤ key

3. Listen and fill in the blanks.

① a wide selection of cars

② include insurance

③ has a lot of miles

④ for 2 days

⑤ passport

⑥ Chinese driver's license

⑦ return the car

⑧ return cars in different cities

⑨ finish filling out the form

⑩ guarantor's ID card

Script:

A: Good morning. How can I help you?

B: I want to rent a car.

A: We have a wide selection of cars you can choose from. What kind of cars do you prefer, a compact or SUV?

B: I am here to travel with my girlfriend. I want her to have a good time.

A: Oh. You may have a Benz like this.

B: It must be very expensive. How about the price?

A: It's 50 yuan per day.

B: It's cheap! Does the price include insurance?

A: Yes, of course.

B: But how can you do that?

A: Because this car has a lot of miles on it.

B: But it almost looks new. I like it.

A: So you will take the Benz then, sir.

B: Yes. I'd like to rent it for 2 days.

A: OK. May I have your passport and Chinese driver's license, please.

B: Here you are.

A: Thank you.

B: Where should I return the car?

A: You have to return it here.

B: While in America we can return cars in different cities.

A: I'm sorry about that. But this car must be returned to this lot.

B: Never mind. Where is the key?

A: You have to first finish filling out the form and show me your guarantor's ID card. And the key is on the car, you can take it when you pick the car tomorrow.

B: That's fine.

Module 11　Shopping in Tourism

Task 1　Souvenirs

1. Special terms.

(1) Put the following into English.

① traditional Chinese painting　　② water color painting

③ cursive hand　　④ the four treasures of the study

⑤ ivory carving

⑥ tri-colored glazed pottery of the Tang dynasty

⑦ painted pottery　　⑧ cloisonné vase

⑨ sandal wood fan　　⑩ embroidery

(2) Put the following into Chinese.

① 紫砂壶　　② 贝雕画　　③ 鼻烟壶　　④ 泥塑　　⑤ 脱胎漆器

⑥ 珠绣　　⑦ 绣花　　⑧ 春联　　⑨ 素描　　⑩ 真品

2. Complete the following dialogue.

① There is a big department store just a few blocks away

② What size do you wear

③ How do you like these

④ I was wondering if you could help me

⑤ It's very kind of you to say so

⑥ these shirts are fine

⑦ I would recommend the purple one

⑧ wash it in lukewarm water and don't rub it

3. Listen and fill in the blanks.

① kill some time ② exhausted

③ energetic ④ hot spring bath

⑤ massage ⑥ snacks

Script:

Mr. Baker asks Wang Hui whether there's anything he could do to kill some time. Although his parents are exhausted after the tour, he is still energetic. Then Wang Hui advises him to have a hot spring bath. There's bath and massage in the hotel. Besides, they provide snacks and drinks for the tourists to choose from.

Task 2 Arts and Crafts

1. Listen and fill in the blanks.

① souvenirs ② fragile ③ heavy

④ combs ⑤ handicrafts ⑥ recommend

Script:

Shop Assistant: Good afternoon, sir. May I help you?

Mr. Brown: Yes. I'd like to buy some special local souvenirs for my family.

Shop Assistant: OK. How about some porcelain?

Mr. Brown: Well, that's rather fragile.

Shop Assistant: Don't worry. We'll have it wrapped.

Mr. Brown: Thanks, but I have a long way to get home. Besides, they look too heavy.

Shop Assistant: I see. How about some wooden products, then? There are many wooden products in our shop.

Mr. Brown: That would be fine.

Shop Assistant: All the wooden are in this section: wood sculptures, wooden chopsticks, and so on.

Mr. Brown: These combs look nice! How much are they?

Shop Assistant: 300 yuan. Ladies usually like them.

Mr. Brown: I agree. I'll take these two.

Shop Assistant: OK. I'll wrap them up for you. Would you like anything else. For example some handicrafts or local delicacies?

Mr. Brown: Could you recommend some gifts for children or the elderly?

Shop Assistant: Sure. These jade talismans and bracelets are quite nice. They make good gifts for children or the elderly.

Mr. Brown: Good. I'll take some.

2. Translate the following sentences into Chinese.

① 先拨国际直拨通话代号011，加上你的国家代码86和你要拨打的手机号码。如果是座机,还要在你想要拨打的座机号码前加上区号。这样你就可以打通到中国的越洋电话了。

② 如果您要给本城的人打电话,可以直接从您的房间打。您需要先按0,等听到提示音后再按您所要的号码。如果需要的话,您也可以打由对方付费的电话。

3. Translate the following sentences into English.

① Fujian bodiless lacquer ware and the cloisonné of Beijing, the porcelain of Jingdezhen, are reputed as three renowned traditional handicrafts in China.

② Chinese traditional painting is highly regarded throughout the world for its long history, original style and distinctive national features.

③ Chinese stitchery is beautifully patterned and exquisitely embroidered.

④ The arts and crafts of China are many and varied in categories.

⑤ The sandal wood fans are not only for ornamental purpose but also for practical use.

Task 3　Tea

1. Complete the following dialogue in English with the information given.

① By the way, would you like to take some leather bags home

② I'm just offering a shopping opportunity and you're by no means obligated to buy anything

③ This store offers ice tea as well. Free of charge

④ About forty minutes, I suppose. Do you think that's enough

⑤ They sure do, at least sufficient enough to get their jobs done

3. Put the following Chinese into English.

① It has to be kept in mind that the major interest of most tourists is usually in sightseeing instead of shopping. Therefore, avoid making frequent shopping arrangements lest the tourists should be tired and protest.

② To be more competitive in the market, travel agencies usually pay tourist guides rather poorly, which makes tips and commission on top of the salary almost the only means for guides to acquire a relatively favorable income.

4. Listen and fill in the blanks.

① temple fair   ② traced   ③ associated   ④ rituals

⑤ religious   ⑥ commerce   ⑦ folk custom   ⑧ acrobatics

⑨ appreciate   ⑩ lifestyles   ⑪ improvements   ⑫ keep pace with

Script:

During the Spring Festival holidays, visiting a temple fair is one of the most important activities. The history of temple fairs may be traced back to the Yuan dynasty, when they were closely associated with Buddhist or Taoist rituals. The fairs held at the ancient temples, and later became centers of religious worship, entertainment and commerce.

A temple fair is a type of folk custom in China. There are performances such as acrobatics and martial arts, numerous kinds of local snacks and other items. In recent years, the temple fair has become a place for people to appreciate traditional arts and experience traditional lifestyles.

In recent years, there have been over 10 major temple fairs held each year in Beijing. Chinese people still love going to temple fairs held each year in Beijing. Chinese people still love going to temple fairs during the Spring Festival holidays. Organizers are also making improvements to the events to keep pace with the times.

Module 12   Recreational Program

Task 1   Health Activities

1. Translate the following sentences into English.

① The hotel offers a full range of recreational facilities and services.

② The fitness center offers an expansive space decked out with all the latest modern fitness equipment.

③ The fitness center is open to our guests for free.

④ The heated pool is on the 6th floor of the hotel.

⑤ The sauna center on the 7th floor is a good place to relax.

2. Listen to the recording and fill in the blanks of the passage.

① traditional sport   ② representative
③ worldwide   ④ Kung Fu masters
⑤ unique existence   ⑥ influence
⑦ lifestyle   ⑧ from generation to generation
⑨ self-defense   ⑩ fitness

Script:

Chinese Kung Fu

The origins of Chinese Kung Fu can be found over 6,000 years ago, when men were taught to hunt and fight. Nowadays, it is regarded as a traditional sport gaining more and more popularity and even stands as a representative for Chinese culture. Styles including Shaolin, Tai Chi and Qigong have many followers worldwide. Some Westerners think that all Chinese people are Kung Fu masters. That's not true, but this traditional heritage has its unique existence in modern times and left much influence on the locals' lifestyle.

Although being fighting styles, Kung Fu advocates virtue and peace, not aggression or violence. This has been the common value upheld by martial artists from generation to generation. With a number of movement sets, boxing styles, weapon skills and some fighting stunts, Kung Fu keeps its original function of self-defense. Now its value in body-building and fitness is also highly appreciated.

Task 2 Watch Shows

1. Translate the following sentences into English.

① In China, various entertainments such as dancing and singing, operas, comic dialogues, movies, etc., can fully satisfy your eyes and ear's.

② We are going to watch the mask-changing in the theater tonight.

③ Attention, everyone. Please meet together at the lobby of the hotel at 7:30 p.m.

④ It will be a great pity if we don't enjoy Beijing Opera when traveling in China.

⑤ Chinese acrobatic performance is one of the favorite arts for Chinese people.

2. Listen to the recording and fill in the blanks of the passage.

① Chinese opera　　　　② earthy quality

③ as early as　　　　　 ④ Qing dynasty

⑤ two roles　　　　　　⑥ female role

⑦ short plays　　　　　 ⑧ performers

⑨ props　　　　　　　　⑩ dialect

Script:

Hunan Flower Drum Opera

Hunan Huaguxi, literally known as Hunan Flower Drum Opera, is a form of Chinese opera originating in Hunan Province. It is known in China for its earthy quality, and is often referred to as the "spicy" form of Chinese opera. Huaguxi is known to have existed as early as 1695, during the Qing dynasty. Unlike other forms of Chinese opera, Huaguxi originally had only two roles. These including xiaochou, a small male clown, and xiaodan, a vivacious young girl. The female role was played by men until women entered Chinese opera in the early 20th century. In the mid-18th century, a xiaosheng role was added. This role refers to handsome young males.

Most Huaguxi plays were originally xiaoxi, short plays lasting an hour or less. These plays often dealt with everyday rural life. With the rise of professional Huaguxi performers and performances in the capital city of Changsha, longer plays, daxi, began to be performed. These plays dealt with grander themes of social satire and class struggle. Like other forms of Chinese opera, Huaguxi is staged with very few props. Music accompanying Huaguxi reflects the Changsha dialect spoken in Hunan. It is played with instruments like datong (fiddle), yueqin (moon lute), dizi (bamboo flute), and suona (oboe). Percussion instruments provide the basic tempo for the performance.

Task 3　Pubs and Bars

1. Translate the following sentences into English.

① Pubs, like cafes in America and tea-houses in China, are an inevitable part of British life and local culture.

② Literally, pubs in the UK are divided into pubs, bars and clubs. Pubs are the common type, enjoying the longest history among them.

③ British pubs can be dated back to over one thousand years ago.

④ Customs in British pubs differ from those in American bars.

⑤ The most popular kind of British beer is bitter, which is dark and served at room temperature.

2. Listen to the recording and fill in the blanks of the passage.

① short for   ② relax   ③ quieter   ④ garden   ⑤ parents

⑥ queue   ⑦ staff   ⑧ by accident   ⑨ soft drinks   ⑩ litres

Script:

What is a Pub?

The word pub is short for public house. There are over 60,000 pubs in the UK. Pubs are an important part of British life. People talk, eat, drink, meet their friends and relax there. Pubs often have two bars, one usually quieter than the other, many have a garden where people can sit in the summer. Children can go in pub gardens with their parents.

Groups of friends normally buy "rounds" of drinks, where the person whose turn it is will buy drinks for all the members of the group. It is sometimes difficult to get served when pubs are busy: people do not queue, but the bar staff will usually try and serve those who have been waiting the longest at the bar first. If you spill a stranger's drink by accident, it is good manners and prudent to offer to buy another drink. Most pubs offer a complete range of beers, local and imported, with German, Belgian and French beers being in demand.

Although most people think pubs are places where people drink alcohol, pubs in fact sell soft drinks too. British people drink an average of 99.4 litres of beer every year. More than 80% of this beer is drunk in pubs and clubs.

Task 4 Traditional Chinese Entertainment

1. Translate the following sentences into English.

① The Chinese lion dance is sometimes mistakenly referred to as the dragon dance.

② The dance of a lion is preformed by two performers, one at the head of the lion, the other at the tail of the lion.

③ This lion dance is life-like.

④ The lion dance is meant to bring fortune and happiness to the people in the new year to come.

⑤ Lion dances are mainly divided into the Northern lion dance and the Southern lion dance.

2. Listen to the recording and fill in the blanks of the passage.

① wisdom　　② associated with　　③ horns　　④ scales　　⑤ performed

⑥ drum　　⑦ knowledge　　⑧ length　　⑨ lucky　　⑩ torch

Script:

Dragon Dances

Dragons are of course legendary animals, but they are important to Chinese people who think of dragons as helpful, friendly creatures. They are linked to good luck, long life and wisdom. They are nothing like the fierce, fire-breathing Western dragons that carry off princesses and eat people. Chinese dragons are associated with storm clouds and life-giving rain. They have special power so they can fly in the air, swim in the sea and walk on land. The dragon has features of other animals such as the horns of a stag, the scales of a fish and the footpads of a tiger.

Dragon dances are performed at New Year to scare away evil spirits. During the dance the performers hold poles and raise and lower the dragon. Sometimes one man has a "Pearl of Wisdom" on a pole and he entices the dragon to follow him to the beat of a drum, as if searching for wisdom and knowledge.

Dragons used in dragon dances vary in length from a few meters to up to 100 m long. Longer dragons are thought to be more lucky than shorter ones. The dances can be performed either during the day or night, but at night a blazing torch will be carried to light the way.

Module 13　Seeing off Guests

Task 1　Checking Out

1. Matching.

① b　　② f　　③ a　　④ c　　⑤ e　　⑥ d

2. Phrases interpreting.

问询处	inquiry office; information counter	一行 25 人	a party of twenty-five
退房	check out	登机牌	boarding check
托运	to book or check through	行李箱	suitcase
候机室	airport lounge	登机	boarding
起飞时间	departure time	安检	safety inspection

3. Discuss and write down.

① If you are a local guide, what preparation should be done before seeing off the guests?

First: Verify the tickets. Verify the departure flight. Make sure: the name of the group, the code, number of the tourists, the name of the national guide, the destination, the flight number, the departure time, and the airport.

Second: Decide the time to collect the luggage.

Third: Decide the time to leave and the place to meet.

Fourth: Decide the time for the wake-up call and breakfast.

Fifth: Assist the hotel to check out.

Sixth: Return the documents.

② What can you do to help the tourist group to check out?

First help them confirm by carefully checking and then collect the room cards and go to the hotel to check every room one by one and then pay the bill and finally leave.

4. Listen and fill in the blanks.

① are all the tourists of the group here

② Thank you

③ And did everybody take his room card and luggage

④ OK, it is great. After checking out, we can leave now

⑤ How about this trip

⑥ I need to count the number of our group and the number of luggage again and then we can go to the bus to leave

⑦ please take your luggage together and then we can move them to the bus

⑧ Yes, please get on the bus now

Script:

(A=the guide   B=the tour leader)

A:Excuse me, are all the tourists of the group here?

B:Let me check it.

A:Thank you.

B:Yes, all the members are here.

A:And did everybody take his room card and luggage?

B:OK. Let us count again.

A:OK, it is great. After checking out, we can leave now.

B:Hello, everybody, let's get on the bus.

B:And great thanks to the guide. Thank you for meeting us.

A:I'm glad to be of service, Miss Smith. Welcome to Fuzhou again. How about this trip?

B:I'm glad to say we all love Fuzhou after this trip.

A:That's great. However, I need to count the number of our group and the number of luggage again and then we can go to the bus to leave.

B:Thank you again.

A:Now, please take your luggage together and then we can move them to the bus.

B:OK. Here you are. There are 16 pieces altogether.

A:Yes, please get on the bus now.

B:I'm glad to hear that. Shall we go now?

A:Yes, of course.

Task 2   Extending a Farewell Speech

1. Discuss and write down.

① What attitude should a guide take in settling departure issues and saying farewell to his/her guests?

  a. Be very considerate and responsible when arranging the departure.

  b. Confirm all needed departure information beforehand and think carefully about all details such as luggage pickup and early check-out, etc.

c. Give assistance as much as possible during the whole departure, as the foreign tourists are normally unfamiliar with China's airport and customs regulation.

d. Be helpful and friendly as possible.

② Where should the tour guide deliver the farewell speech? What information should a farewell speech deliver?

Where: During the last dinner, the way to the airport or railway station, at the airport or railway station

Main elements of a farewell speech: Express the feeling of parting, thanks for co-operation; make a conclusion to the trip; make apologies if there is inadequacy in service; extend best wishes

2. Listen and fill in the blanks.

① goes　　　② drawing　　　③ any longer　　　④ great

⑤ cooperation　⑥ old　　　⑦ brings　　　⑧ memories

⑨ back　　　⑩ Once again

Script:

Ladies and Gentlemen:

Time goes quickly and your trip in Wuhan is drawing to a close. It's a pity that you cannot stay in our country any longer. Then allow me to take this opportunity to say goodbye to you.

I would like to tell you that it is a great pleasure for me to be your guide these days. I have had the opportunity to meet and get to know you. Thank you for the cooperation and support you gave us in the past several days. As a Chinese old saying goes, "A good friend from afar brings a distant land closer." I hope you'll take happy memories of your trip in China back home.

I wish to see you again in the future and to be your guide. Once again, thank you for your cooperation and support.

Goodbye!

3. Translation.

① 与客人道别意味着导游服务的结束。无论道别安排在什么地方，它都与欢迎同等重要，应该真诚地进行。在这最后一刻，如果有任何不愉快发生，都会毁掉整个旅途体验。因此，一个合格的导游应该尽力提供一次令人难忘的、永恒的经历。

② If the farewell arrangements are made properly, a successful stop can be given to the whole work of a tour guide. Otherwise, it may cause delays or other problems to the guests' next itinerary and ruin all previous efforts.

Task 3 Departure Procedure

1. Translation.

① 团体签证   ② 起飞

③ 出境签证   ④ 出境游客休息室

⑤ 行李架   ⑥ 母婴休息室

⑦ security check   ⑧ charge for overweight

⑨ customs dealer   ⑩ free luggage

⑪ return ticket   ⑫ boarding gate

⑬ tourist class   ⑭ boarding card (pass)

2. Complete the following dialogues in English with the information given.

① Has everybody checked out

② Please make sure that you do not leave anything behind

③ It has been my pleasure

④ The stay with you is also a happy thing for me. I do wish you a safe and pleasant journey back home

⑤ Hope you'll visit Beijing again

⑥ Sure. Please give my best regards to your family

⑦ Thank you for your compliments

⑧ Oh, it is time for you to get in. We have to say goodbye now

⑨ Good-bye. Hope to see you in the future

3. Listen and fill in the blanks.

① say goodbye to you

② nothing lasts forever

③ kindness

④ come to China again.

⑤ I'm glad to hear that

⑥ journey

Script:

(G=the guide   T=the tourist)

G:Hello, Mr. Brown. It is time for me to say goodbye to you.

T:Yes, we have to. It is hard to tear myself away from you and your friendly people, but nothing lasts forever. I have to go back home soon. Thank you very much for your kindness. I will always remember you.

G:I hope you will come to China again.

T:I hope so. I am sure I will return soon. I will tell you a piece of good news. I was invited to be a visiting professor to teach at Hunan University for a year.

G:I'm glad to hear that.

T:Good-bye. Please say hello to your family for me.

G:A happy journey home.

T:Good-bye. See you next year.

References

[1] 王月等. 体验旅游英语[M]. 北京:中国水利水电出版社,2008.

[2] 张静慧. 涉外旅游与酒店情景英语[M]. 青岛:中国海洋大学出版社,2011.

[3] 吴云,吴文婷. 旅游实践英语[M]. 2版. 北京:旅游教育出版社,2013.

[4] 黎晓伟,陆正刚. 旅游服务英语实训[M]. 2版. 北京:对外经济贸易大学出版社,2014.

[5] 李晓红. 旅游英语综合教程[M]. 北京:中国人民大学出版社,2014.

[6] 朱岐新. 英语导游必读[M]. 北京:中国旅游出版社,2005.

[7] 安福勇,毛春洲,徐丽娜. 实用导游英语[M]. 武汉:华中科技大学出版社,2011.

[8] 冯玮. 新编导游英语[M]. 2版. 武汉:武汉大学出版社,2007.

[9] 陆建平. 现代旅游英语教程[M]. 北京:商务印书馆,2008.

[10] 浩瀚,李生禄. 旅游英语实战实例[M]. 北京:北京航空航天大学出版社,2009.

[11] 导游资格证考试导游实务口试四十道题[OL/D]. http://www.docin.com/p-287084526.html.

[12] Tips for Tour Guide[OL/D]. https://wenku.baidu.com/view/447a9c95c1c708a1284a445a.html.

[13] Unit 2 On the Way to the Hotel. [OL/D] http://www.doc88.com/p-187690358004.html.

[14] Hunan Travel Guide [OL/D]. http://www.topchinatravel.com/hunan/.

[15] Changsha Travel Guide [OL/D]. https://www.chinahighlights.com/changsha/.

[16] 吴淑娟,王纯阳.旅游英语实用教程[M].北京:北京大学出版社,2016.

[17] 程丛喜.实用旅游英语听说教程[M].武汉:武汉大学出版社,2012.

[18] 郑毅,刘惠波.旅游英语视听说[M].北京:外语教学与研究出版社,2011.

[19] 孙小珂.旅游专业英语[M].武汉:武汉大学出版社,2001.

[20] 莫红英.旅游基础英语[M]北京:旅游教育出版社,2007.

[21] The Top 10 Attractions in China [OL/D].
https://www.chinahighlights.com/travelguide/china-top-10-attractions.htm.

[22] Zhangjiajie Tours [OL/D].
https://www.chinahighlights.com/zhangjiajie/tours.htm.

[23] World Heritage Sites in China [OL/D].
https://www.chinahighlights.com/travelguide/world-heritage/.

[24] 6 Most Beautiful Mountains in China [OL/D].
https://www.chinahighlights.com/travelguide/famous-mountains.htm.

[25] Changsha Transportation[OL/D].
https://www.chinahighlights.com/changsha/transportation.htm.

[26] Chinese Jade Articles [OL/D].
https://www.chinahighlights.com/travelguide/culture/jade-articles.htm.

[27] Chinese Embroidery [OL/D].
https://www.chinahighlights.com/travelguide/culture/embroidery.htm.

[28] Chinese Porcelain [OL/D].
https://www.chinahighlights.com/travelguide/culture/china-porcelain.htm.

[29] 刘丽莉.导游英语实用教程[M].天津:天津大学出版社,2010.

[30] 牛白琳.导游情景英语[M].2版.北京:高等教育出版社,2010.

[31] http://projectbritain.com/pubs.htm.

[32] http://www.nationsonline.org/oneworld/Chinese_Customs/lion_dance.htm.

[33] https://en.wikipedia.org/wiki/Lion_dance#Costumes.

[34] http://www.bangli.uk/7076.html.

[35] https://www.topmarks.co.uk/ChineseNewYear/DragonDance.aspx.

[36] https://www.travelchinaguide.com/essential/holidays/dragon-boat/

races. htm.

[37] 陈欣.导游英语情景口语[M].北京:北京大学出版社,2010.

[38] 关肇远.导游英语口语[M].2版.北京:高等教育出版社,2009.

[39] 易玉婷,汪锋.英语导游实务——导游业务部分[M].北京:国防工业出版社,2012.

[40] 朱华.导游英语[M].2版.北京:高等教育出版社,2013.

[41] 袁智敏,仉向明.领队英语[M].5版.北京:旅游教育出版社,2016.

[42] https://www.gov.uk/foreign-travel-advice/china/health.

[43] https://www.chinahighlights.com/travelguide/guidebook/emergencies.htm.

[44] https://www.travelchinaguide.com/essential/emergency.htm.

[45] 雷兵.酒店英语听说实训教程[M].北京:科学出版社,2009.

[46] 卢凤萍,姜丽娟.导游情景英语[M].南京:南京大学出版社,2015.

教学支持说明

一流高职院校旅游大类创新型人才培养"十三五"规划教材系华中科技大学出版社"十三五"规划重点教材。

为了改善教学效果,提高教材的使用效率,满足高校授课教师的教学需求,本套教材备有与纸质教材配套的教学课件(PPT 电子教案)和拓展资源(案例库、习题库、视频等)。

为保证本教学课件及相关教学资料仅为教材使用者所得,我们将向使用本套教材的高校授课教师免费赠送教学课件或者相关教学资料,烦请授课教师通过电话、邮件或加入旅游专家俱乐部 QQ 群等方式与我们联系,获取"教学课件资源申请表"文档并认真准确填写后发给我们,我们的联系方式如下:

地址:湖北省武汉市东湖新技术开发区华工科技园华工园六路

邮编:430223

电话:027-81321911

传真:027-81321917

E-mail:lyzjjlb@163.com

旅游专家俱乐部 QQ 群号:306110199

旅游专家俱乐部 QQ 群二维码:

群名称:旅游专家俱乐部
群　号:306110199

教学课件资源申请表

填表时间：_____年___月___日

1. 以下内容请教师按实际情况填写，★为必填项。
2. 学生根据个人情况如实填写，相关内容可以酌情调整提交。

★姓名		★性别	□男 □女	出生年月		★职务	
						★职称	□教授 □副教授 □讲师 □助教
★学校				★院/系			
★教研室				★专业			
★办公电话		家庭电话				★移动电话	
★E-mail （请填写清晰）						★QQ号/微信号	
★联系地址						★邮编	

★现在主授课程情况	学生人数	教材所属出版社	教材满意度
课程一			□满意 □一般 □不满意
课程二			□满意 □一般 □不满意
课程三			□满意 □一般 □不满意
其 他			□满意 □一般 □不满意

教材出版信息		
方向一		□准备写 □写作中 □已成稿 □已出版待修订 □有讲义
方向二		□准备写 □写作中 □已成稿 □已出版待修订 □有讲义
方向三		□准备写 □写作中 □已成稿 □已出版待修订 □有讲义

请教师认真填写表格下列内容，提供索取课件配套教材的相关信息，我社根据每位教师/学生填表信息的完整性、授课情况与索取课件的相关性，以及教材使用的情况赠送教材的配套课件及相关教学资源。

ISBN（书号）	书名	作者	索取课件简要说明	学生人数 （如选作教材）
			□教学 □参考	
			□教学 □参考	

★您对与课件配套的纸质教材的意见和建议，希望提供哪些配套教学资源：